Fun Accessories
to Sew for Your Dog

D1299675

BOOK SOLD
NO LONGER R. H.P.L.
PROPERTY

Fun Accessories to Sew for Your Dog

by Jisu Lee (Tingk)

Copyright © 2013, 2018 Sigongsa Co., Ltd.

All rights reserved.
Originally published in Korea by Sigongsa Co., Ltd.
English translation copyright © 2018 New Design Originals Corporation
Arranged with Sigongsa Co., Ltd. through LEE's Literary Agency, Taiwan

Fun Accessories to Sew for Your Dog is an abridged translation of the original Korean language book. This version published by CompanionHouse Books, an imprint of Fox Chapel Publishers International Ltd.

Project Team for English Version
Vice President–Content: Christopher Reggio
Editor: Amy Deputato
Copy Editor: Kaitlyn Ocasio
Design: Mary Ann Kahn

ISBN 978-1-62187-179-8

The Cataloging-in-Publication Data has been applied for.

This book has been published with the intent to provide accurate and authoritative information in regard to the subject matter within. While every precaution has been taken in the preparation of this book, the author and publisher expressly disclaim any responsibility for any errors, omissions, or adverse effects arising from the use or application of the information contained herein.

Fox Chapel Publishing
903 Square Street
Mount Joy, PA 17552

Fox Chapel Publishers International Ltd.
7 Danefield Road, Selsey (Chichester)
West Sussex PO20 9DA, U.K.

www.facebook.com/companionhousebooks

We are always looking for talented authors. To submit an idea, please send a brief inquiry to acquisitions@foxchapelpublishing.com.

Printed and bound in China
21 20 19 18   2 4 6 8 10 9 7 5 3 1

RICHMOND HILL PUBLIC LIBRARY
32972001120825   OR
Fun accessories to sew for your dog : 23
Oct. 17, 2018

Fun Accessories to Sew for Your Dog

23 Cool Things to Make for Your Dog

Contents

 **Part 1**

Essential Tips and Techniques

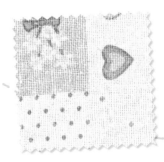

Part 2

Projects

Introduction

Making One-of-a-Kind Adorable Clothes for Your Dogs!

In the year I got married, our dogs Furryhead and Gucci joined our family and started to bond deeply with us. Seeing them growing up day by day, I had the desire to make them some clothes on my own. In the beginning I was all thumbs and made lousy products. I felt totally satisfied, however, when I saw Furryhead and Gucci putting on my handmade clothes and happily playing around. Time flies—Furryhead and Gucci have been with us for ten years now. My pet-clothes-making skills are also getting better and better.

Many people might think it is good enough to buy their dogs' clothes and accessories in animal hospitals or pet stores. However, each dog is unique and might not fit in mass-produced clothing. Nowadays, more and more people are aware of this fact and willingly take out their sewing kits to make pet clothes on their own. In order to help these people, in this book I have shared all my experiences and methodologies for making pet clothes as much as possible. The method for making pet clothes is very similar to that for making human clothes. The biggest difference is that the body shape of pets is very different from that of human beings. Therefore, you need to understand the body formation and characteristics of your pets before making pet clothes for them. In the beginning, you might encounter some setbacks. Don't worry. Just keep going with love and care for your pets. I believe you can make very unique and lovely pet clothes for your pets!

I would like to thank many people for helping me along the way with this book. First off, I would like to thank my family for their continuous support. I also want to express my sincere gratitude to all the staff, sewing masters, cute dog models, and their owners who contributed their efforts and made this book possible. My special thanks go to Sigongsa Co. Ltd., Miss Ji Yoon, the photographers, and the art designers who made this book such a beautiful publication. Of course, I won't forget those online friends who cheer me up on my blogs. Thank you all!

Last but not least, I hope this book can become a stepping-stone for you to learn sewing. For those readers who think it is very difficult to sew pet clothes, I hope you can challenge yourself with confidence after reading this book!

Tingk

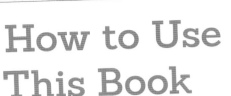

How to Use This Book

Each project in this book is presented with every detail necessary to create the project, even for a novice sewer.

A. Opening each project are model shots of a happy dog wearing the completed projects. These shots are a handy reference when you are putting together your project. They help you see what you're aiming to create and how the piece should fit your dog.

B. Each project's instructions section starts off with the essentials you need to know. These include the finished size of the project used for the instructions, the amount and type of fabric you'll need to buy, and a list of additional notions you'll need, like buttons, interfacing, and other bits and pieces.

C. Next, you see the pattern pieces and their essential measurements so that you can cut out all your pieces. Some rectangular pieces you can measure and cut yourself.

D. Finally, you can follow the clear photographs, illustrations, and step-by-step instructions to put together your selected project. Tips throughout help ensure that you don't miss a detail.

Essential Tips
and Techniques

Part 1

Before You Begin

Understand the lengthwise and crosswise grain

While sewing, the selvage edge marks the lengthwise (vertical) grain of the fabric. This grain is more stable, so fabric should be cut along the lengthwise grain. A simple way to find the orientation of the fabric is to pull it. The lengthwise grain offers no elasticity while the crosswise (horizontal) grain has a bit of give. The fabric widths mentioned in this book and at your local fabric store refer to the horizontal width of the fabric. Make sure you are purchasing the right yardage for the specific width you find when gathering your supplies.

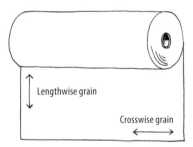

Lengthwise grain

Crosswise grain

Wash your fabric

Before you use your fabric, make sure to wash it so it preshrinks and behaves more like the natural fiber. To wash your fabric, soak it in warm water for 1 to 2 hours. Agitate it several times and then wring it out. Put it in a shady, cool place to air dry and then iron it when it is nearly dry.

Iron your fabric

Before you cut your fabric, I suggest that you iron it. Ironing your fabric before using it can improve the finished look. You should also iron your fabric at every step in the sewing process to finish the seams and make the completed project look more professional.

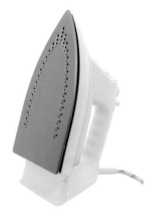

Ways to cut your fabric

Unfolded fabric:

- Spread out the fabric with the wrong side up. Lay out the pattern pieces with the grain line aligned with the selvage edge. Trace the pattern onto the fabric with marking tools, such as water-soluble pens, disappearing ink pens, or tailor's chalk.

- Trace around the pattern pieces for one side and then flip the pattern over to draw the remaining side.

- When flipping the pattern, make sure that the center marking is aligned. If the pattern calls for a center seam, make sure that the necessary seam allowances are marked.

- Draw the necessary seam allowances with a seam gauge and then cut out the pattern pieces.

Half-folded fabric:

- Lay the pattern pieces on the half-folded fabric and then trace the pattern.

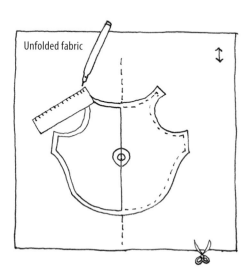

Unfolded fabric

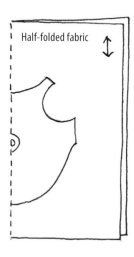

Half-folded fabric

How to Make Clothes for Your Dog

Measure your dog

Before you start making pet clothes, you need to know your dog's neck and chest circumferences. Because there might be measurement errors due to the dog's postures and different reference points, you need to confirm the measurements repeatedly according to the types of clothes you want to make.

Tips for measuring your dog

- Avoid measuring your dog while he leans to one side or looks down.

- Measure your dog while he stretches his back. Repeat several times and take an average.

- Avoid getting too tight or too loose when using the tape measure.

- Add a bit of extra length when measuring shaggy dogs.

- The chart on page 13 is based on the dog's body length. The patterns in this book also follow this chart. You can use it as a reference to choose the patterns that best fit your dog.

- Using the same pattern with different fabrics might result in different sizes of the finished clothes. If you use thick materials like wools, be sure to add ¾ –1¼ inches (2–3 cm) to the original patterns. On the other hand, if using knit fabric, you should subtract ⅜ inch (1 cm) from the original patterns.

- The size of the front pieces will vary due to the dog's gender. For female dogs, you can make the front pieces a bit shorter.

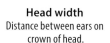

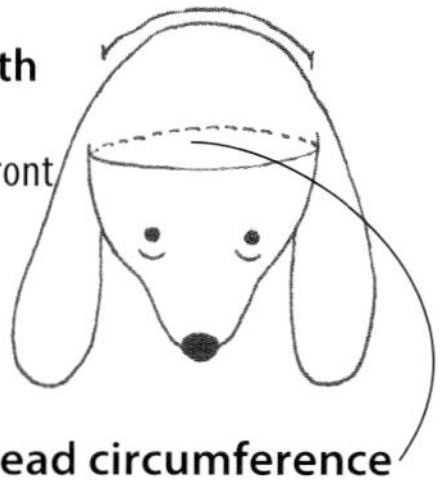

Head width
Distance between ears on crown of head.

Head length
(horizontal)
Measure on front of head.

Head circumference
(horizontal) From top of ears making a circle through forehead.

Head circumference (vertical) From chin to top of head, in front of ears.

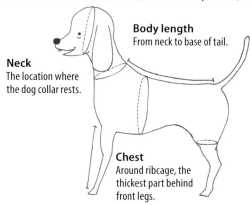

Body length
From neck to base of tail.

Neck
The location where the dog collar rests.

Chest
Around ribcage, the thickest part behind front legs.

Dog Clothing Size Chart (based on body length)

Size	Neck	Chest	Back length
XS	7½ inches (19 cm)	11 inches (28 cm)	8¾ inches (22 cm)
S	8¾ inches (22 cm)	12¾ inches (32 cm)	9¾ inches (25 cm)
M	9¾ inches (25 cm)	14½ inches (37 cm)	10½ inches (27 cm)
L	11½ inches (29 cm)	16½ inches (42 cm)	11½ inches (29 cm)
XL	13 inches (33 cm)	19 inches (48 cm)	13 inches (33 cm)

Dog Hat Size Chart (based on body length)

Size	Head (horizontal)	Head (vertical)
S	8¼ –9¾ inches (21–25 cm)	8¼ –9¾ inches (21–25 cm)
M	10¼–11¾ inches (26–30 cm)	10¼ –11¾ inches (26–30 cm)
L	12¼ –13¾ inches (31–35 cm)	12¼ –13¾ inches (31–35 cm)

Find your pattern

Different kinds of dogs have different body types and sizes. Therefore, it is impossible to have one-size-fits-all clothing for dogs. Before you copy and adjust the pattern, be sure you understand your dog's physical characteristics.

If the pattern fits…

- If any size (XS, S, M, L, XL) pattern from this book fits your dog, you can copy the pattern onto tracing paper or any other transparent paper.

- Glue the pattern to cardboard to help you cut it out and to keep it in place while you cut your fabric.

If the pattern doesn't fit…

- First, you need to know the differences between your dog's size and the chart on page 13, including chest circumference, neck circumference, and back length.

- Follow the instructions for "How to alter the pattern" on page 16 to change the size.

Making muslins and basting

Before making the actual garment, you can make a sample (muslin) first from scrap fabric or cast-off clothes to make sure the pattern fits. After adding the seam allowances, cut the pattern along the cutting line. Baste along the seam lines and then try the muslin on your dog. If it doesn't fit, find out which part you need to alter for the pattern. Basting not only helps you reduce waste but also makes sewing with the final fabric an easier process.

Cut

Lay the pattern pieces on the wrong side of your fabric and trace the patterns. You will begin to see how the garment looks after stitching up all the pattern pieces. Remember to add seam allowances outside of the seam lines from the pattern. After drawing the seam lines and allowances, you can cut the fabric along the cutting lines and then get to sewing.

The pattern arrangements found on the project instructions pages are meant to conveniently illustrate the pattern pieces you need and in what fabrics. This isn't necessarily the exact pattern layout: you should judge and lay the patterns carefully to waste as little fabric as possible.

Sew

When sewing your dog clothes, you can either use a sewing machine or sew by hand. In my opinion, the best way is to use both methods. It is better to use a sewing machine for large clothes, but sewing by hand is preferred for details and textures. For fabric that unravels easy along the raw edges, I suggest finishing the edges with the overlock function of the sewing machine, or you can hand sew overcast stitches if you don't have a sewing machine.

Confirm the pattern size

The illustration below is an example of a half-folded pattern. Use a tape measure to check the size on each part, compare it to your dog's measurements, and decide whether you need to alter the pattern.

- Neck circumference = (back neck circumference/2 + front neck circumference/2) x 2
- Chest circumference = (chest circumference/2) x 2
- Back length = back length
- Arm hole = arm hole
- Hem length = (hem length/2) x 2

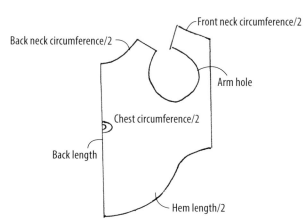

Front neck circumference/2

Back neck circumference/2

Arm hole

Chest circumference/2

Back length

Hem length/2

How to alter the pattern

No matter whether you want to make the pattern longer or shorter, you need to change the size of each pattern piece evenly.

1. If you need to lengthen both the chest and neck circumferences: Add width to the center front and back lines, or vertically cut the neckline open and spread it out (known as slashing and spreading).

2. If you need to shorten both the chest and neck circumferences: Trim the width of the center front and back lines, or vertically cut the neckline open and overlap the cut pieces to reduce the length.

3. If you need to lengthen both the chest circumference and the arm hole: Add width to the side seams of the front and back pieces, or slash and spread the arm hole.

4. If you need to shorten both the chest circumference and the arm hole: Trim the side seams, reducing the width of the front and back pieces, or vertically cut the armhole open and overlap the cut pieces to reduce the length.

5. If you need to lengthen both the neck circumference and the arm hole: Just lengthen the shoulder line.

6. If you need to shorten both the neck circumference and the arm hole: Just reduce the shoulder line.

7. If you need to lengthen the back length: Slash the pattern along the width, right under the arm hole and then spread the cut pieces, adding another layer of paper underneath to bridge the gap.

8. If you need to shorten the back length: Slash the pattern along the width, right under the armhole and then overlap the cut pieces to reduce the length.

9. If you only need to lengthen the neck circumference: Extend the neckline outward and then connect the line back to the shoulder line.

10. If you only need to shorten the neck circumference: Trim the neckline inward, making sure it connects back to the shoulder line.

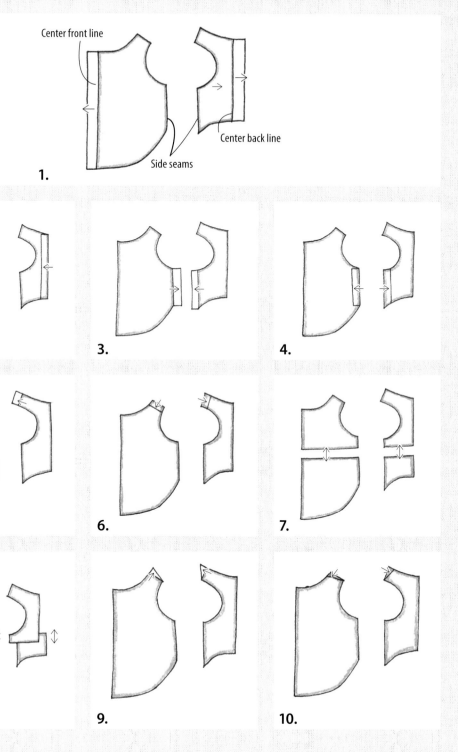

1.

Center front line

Center back line

Side seams

2.

3.

4.

5.

6.

7.

8.

9.

10.

Tools and Materials

1. Seam gauge: A ruler that shows various seam allowances. It is essential for sewing.

2. Stitching awl: To pick out fabric at edges or corners when turning the fabric right side out. Especially helpful for making thin ropes or straps. You can also use it to push or hold your fabric while underneath the sewing machine and protect your fingers.

3. Seam ripper: To rip seams when you make mistakes.

4. Thimble: To protect your fingertips from being poked by needles and to help you push needles easily while sewing with thicker fabric by hand.

5. Scissors: I suggest using dedicated scissors for different things: to cut fabric, use fabric scissors; to cut threads, use thread-cutting scissors.

6. Needles: You will need different sizes of needles for different kinds of fabrics and uses. It's best to collect all kinds of sizes of sewing needles for both hand and machine sewing.

7. Fabric markers: Tools for tracing patterns or to mark size notes on the fabric. The ink of disappearing ink pens will evaporate in the air after a while, while the ink of water-soluble pens can be removed with water.

8. Pins and pincushion: Pins are used to hold fabrics and notions in place while cutting or sewing. A pincushion is just the pin holder, commonly seen in two types: classic cushions and magnetic ones.

9. Iron: To smooth out your fabric or press creases along seam lines. You can iron the fabric before cutting and after finishing sewing.

10. Tape measure: To measure body size and curve lengths.

11. Bone folder: A very convenient tool used to mark seam allowances or fold lines.

12. Tracing wheel: A marking tool used to make dotted lines directly on patterns or fabric.

13. Fabric adhesive: A water-soluble glue for fabric. It can be used to hold fabric pieces together temporarily as a substitute for pins. You can also use it to glue pockets on clothes.

1. Thread: Comes in different types, including cotton and silk threads, and in a variety of colors. I recommend choosing one in a similar material as your fabric and in a color a shade darker than the fabric. Make sure you use hand-sewing threads while sewing by hand since these threads are very strong and do not easily break.

2. Basting threads for quilting: General basting threads break easily, but basting thread for quilting is made from 100% cotton, is soft and doesn't tangle easily, and is a better choice for both quilting and basting.

3. Invisible threads: Transparent and thin, this thread is used to hide stitches.

4. Embroidery threads: Thicker than regular threads, these can be used to embroider patterns or for decorative stitches.

5. Hook-and-loop fastener: A fabric fastener used by sticking the loop side to the hooked side. This makes sizing adjustable in clothing. Velcro also works.

6. Leather cording: Used to decorate bags or accessories.

7. Cotton strings: Used to decorate accessories by tying on beads or by knotting.

8. Elastic: Used to make the size of clothes or hats adjustable. Be sure to pick the proper size according to the project instructions.

9. Loop turner: Used to turn long straps inside out. The handle and hook design makes it very easy to use.

10. Bodkin needle: Used to draw elastic or cotton strings through thin tubes or similar casings.

11. Fusible stay tape: Also known as fusible stabilizing tape, these tapes are available in a wide variety. Choose the proper one according to the fabric you're using and the final use of the finished product. To use it, put the stay tape on top of the fabric with the glue facing down and iron it. The benefit of the stay tape is to prevent curved edges from becoming stretched out or warped. It helps the overall shape of the garment and improves the finished look.

12. Locking forceps: A tool that helps fill projects with batting. It is especially convenient for tucking batting and other fillings into narrow openings.

13. Polyester fiberfill: A kind of filling material that quickly restores to its original shape and doesn't easily bunch after being washed. It is commonly used to fill dolls and accessories.

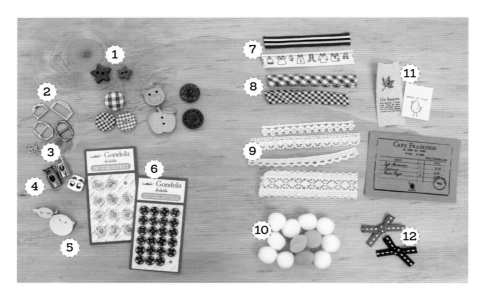

1. Decorative buttons: Available in various styles and materials. You can enhance the look of a finished product.

2. Slide buckles and D-rings: Inserting a belt onto a slide buckle can make the belt length adjustable. Be sure you choose the proper hardware according to your project. D-rings are typically used as joiners on hats or bags, and, unlike slide buckles, you need to sew D-rings into straps or belts.

3. Hook and eye: A hook-and-eye closure is a very simple and secure method of fastening garments together. It can be used on skirts, dresses, cardigans, vests, and capes. There are two parts of this fastening item—a hook and an eye. You need to sew them on as a pair.

4. Spring stopper: The length of your cording can be adjustable after putting it through a spring stopper. They can be made from metal or plastic.

5. Brooch base: You can create a brooch just by gluing some decorative ribbons and buttons onto a brooch base with hot glue adhesive.

6. Invisible snaps: An invisible snap comes in a pair—a prong and socket. They can be used as a substitute for regular buttons, but be sure to confirm the placement before sewing them on.

7. Decorative ribbons: Items to enhance the style of bags and accessories. Don't forget to choose ones that match the material of your project.

8. Bias tape: Available in various sizes and materials, such as linen, cotton and knit. You can choose a suitable one based on your project needs, or you can make them yourself from your own fabric.

9. Lace strips: Suitable for all kinds of fabrics and designs. There are many sizes and patterns. You should keep a variety of them handy.

10. Pom-poms: Available in a wide variety of sizes and colors. They can be used as decorations or as substitutes for buttons.

11. Fabric labels: Sewn on the finished products to make them more recognizable. There are many sizes and patterns. You should keep a variety of them handy.

12. Bows: Suitable for decorating clothes and accessories. You can attach them with stitching or hot glue adhesive.

Fabrics

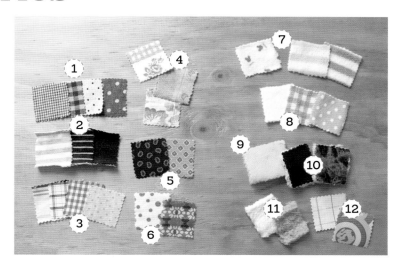

1. Cotton/linen blend: While making pet clothes, it is better to use a cotton/linen blend than 100% pure linen because it is softer and more resilient. When making clothes, washed linen is recommended; when making accessories, you can use thicker linen fabrics.

2. Stretch cotton: Soft and with high absorbency. However, sewing with it is challenging for beginners because it can shift while sewing. Seams can also pop when the fabric stretches, so sewing with a serger (overlocker) is needed.

3. Pure cotton: The yarn count represents the thickness of the threads used for weaving the fabric. The higher the number, the finer the thread is. For dogs with sensitive skin, fabric with a higher count is recommended.

4. Quilting fabric: There are fabrics suitable for quilting available in many stores. It is very convenient to use.

5. Silk: Soft and thin, silk is usually used to make scarves or ties.

6. Cotton Flannel, single and double-napped: Flannelette is famous for its softness, breathability, and absorbability and is commonly used for baby clothes. Double-napped cotton flannel has a nap on both sides of the fabric and is used for handkerchiefs and scarves.

7. Organic terrycloth and terrycloth without opticalbrightener (fluorescent whitening agent): Since there is no chemical added in the production process, this type of fabric is suitable to make clothes and toys for dogs with sensitive skin.

8. Terrycloth: You can choose different thicknesses and loop lengths according to the usage. If you want to make bath products, terrycloth with loops on both sides is recommended.

9. Padded microfiber: Soft and padded, usually used to make cushions and bedding.

10. Leather and denim: These have great stability and are easy to use. You can sew them directly on the right side of the fabric; they often look their best with topstitching.

11. Microfiber double-sided fleece: Soft and comfortable. With fleece on both sides, it is suitable for winter clothes and hats.

12. Double-sided coating fabric: Although it is waterproof, this will still get wet after soaking in water for too long because it is not made of 100 percent polyethylene.

Basic Sewing Terminology

Seam allowance: The width between the seam line and the cutting line marked on the fabric after tracing the pattern.

Edge stitching: A stitch that is sewn on the right side of the outer fabric after stitching it to another piece of fabric. It is a sewing technique that prevents the project from looking bulky, or it is used for decorative purposes. Stitch ¹⁄₁₆- ⅛ inch (0.2–0.3 cm) in from the finished seam. Sew very carefully when doing edge stitching. Sewing further out from the edge, about ¼- ⅜ inch (0.5–1 cm), is known as topstitching.

Opening for turning: A section on the seam line left open for turning the project right side out when the rest of the garment or lining is sewn. The smaller the opening, the better, as long as the project can still be turned inside out. After turning the project right side out, a blind stitch is commonly used to close the opening, or sometimes an edge stitch is used for a decorative seam finish.

Clipping and notching: After sewing the fabric pieces but before turning the project right side out, we usually cut small notches with consistent spacing in the seam allowance to flatten the seam, especially on the curves (for concave curves, clip; for convex curves, notch). To prevent the seam allowances from overlapping, becoming creased, or being too thick, clipping the seam allowance at corners is also recommended. Be careful not to cut into your stitches. If you are using stretch fabrics,

Natural fiberfill and polyester fiberfill
There are two kinds of synthetic fiberfill commercially available: natural fiberfill and polyester fiberfill. Polyester fiberfill has better resilience and fluffiness. It is not easily bunched up, so it is commonly used to fill dolls and accessories. When filling larger projects, such as pillows and cushions, we usually use natural fiberfill. I suggest that you choose the right fiberfill based on the project instructions and the intended use of the finished item.

Natural fiberfill   Polyester fiberfill

you can trim the width of the seam allowance instead of notching and clipping.

Filling: Carefully use the locking forceps to stuff the batting in. When the filling process is almost done, slowly close the opening with blind stitching while pushing in more filling to avoid uneven filling and to ensure a smooth seam finish.

Basic Sewing Techniques

Knotting the thread

  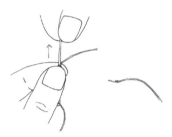

1. Lay the sharp end of the needle on top of one end of the thread.

2. Wrap the thread around the needle two or three times.

3. Grip the wrapped thread with your thumb and index finger. Pull the needle with the other hand while maintaining your grip until the wrapped thread becomes a tight knot.

Basic stitches
Running stitch: Used to stitch two pieces of fabric together or for a decorative topstitch.

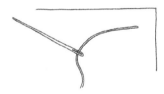  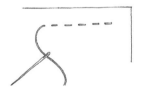

1. After knotting the thread, pull the needle through the fabric from the wrong side to the right side.

2. Make your stitches about 1/16- 1/8 inch (0.2–0.3 cm) apart.

3. Weave your needle in and out for about three to four stitches and then pull the needle all the way through the fabric.

Backstitch: A stronger and more secure stitch than a running stitch.

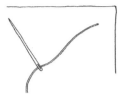

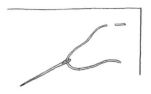

1. After knotting the thread, bring the needle through the fabric to the right side.

2. Make one stitch and then pull the needle through the fabric.

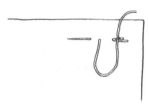

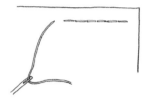

3. Create one more stitch by going back to where the needle emerged previously. Pull the needle through the fabric.

4. Repeat steps 2 and 3.

Overcast stitch: Used as a seam finish to prevent unraveling or as a hem finish.

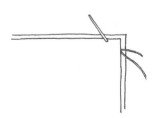

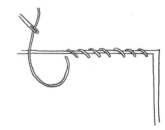

1. After knotting the thread, bring the needle through the fabric to the top edge.

2. Insert the needle diagonally from the inner edge of the fabric and bring it out on the right side.

3. Repeat accordingly until reaching the end. Knot the thread at the end of the stitching line.

Blind stitch: Used to secure hems or to close the opening for turning.

 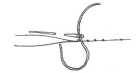 

1. After knotting the thread, insert the needle from the wrong side of the fabric and bring it out on the right side.

2. Pull the thread out and take a stitch on the seam allowance.

3. Don't pull the thread too tight while sewing. Make every effort to ensure that the stitches are hidden inside.

Basting stitch: A temporary stitch to hold the pieces of fabric together or to secure the outer fabric and lining in place before making the actual seam.

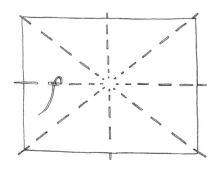

On the fabric, baste along the horizontal, vertical and diagonal lines that cross in the center. There is no need to secure the thread after stitching, but rather leave a 2–2 ⅜ inch (5–6cm) thread tail at the end. After finishing the actual stitches, pull out the basting thread.

Embroidery: Sewing with embroidery and colorful silk threads for decorative purposes.

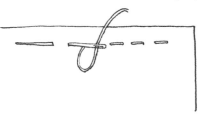

Running stitch: A decorative stitch on the right side of the fabric, same as the running stitch in sewing.

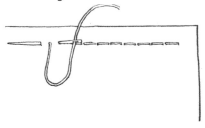

Backstitch: A decorative stitch to show the embroidery threads on the right side, same as the backstitch in sewing.

Seam-finishing techniques

Plain seam finish: Press the seam allowances open for both pieces of the fabric after sewing.

Reversed seam finish: Press the seam allowances of both pieces toward the same side.

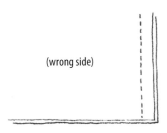

(wrong side)

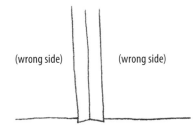

(wrong side)　　　(wrong side)

1. With right sides facing, stitch the two pieces of fabric.

2. Press the seam allowances open and iron them flat.

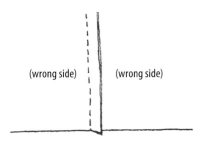

(wrong side)　　(wrong side)

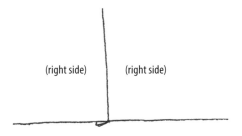

(right side)　　(right side)

1. With right sides facing, stitch the two pieces of fabric.

2. Press both seam allowances toward the same side.

How to prevent unraveling

To prevent unraveling at the fabric edge, you can use the overlock function or zigzag stitches with your sewing machine, or sew overcast stitches by hand.

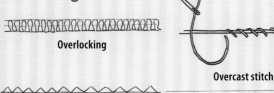

Overlocking

Zigzag stitch

Overcast stitch

Flat fell seam finish: Wrap one side of the seam allowance around the other side and then edge-stitch the fold in place.

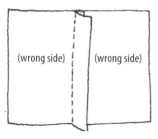

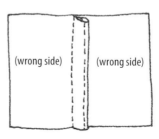

1. After stitching, trim one of the seam allowances.

2. Fold the untrimmed seam allowance, wrap the trimmed seam allowance inside, and press. Edge-stitch the folded edge.

Hem-finishing techniques

Single-fold hem: This is the most basic hem-finishing technique. After the raw edge of the fabric is finished (with overlocking, zigzag, or overcasting stitches), make a single fold and press. Sew the hem in place directly from the right side of the fabric.

Double-fold hem: With this method, the raw edge finish is not needed. Make two folds on the edge of the fabric and then press them in place. Sew the hem in place directly from the right side of the fabric.

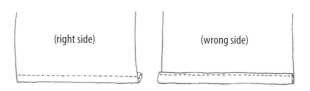

Bound seam finish techniques
Making bias tape

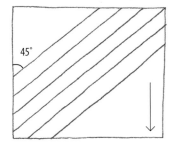

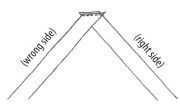

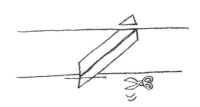

1. On the fabric, draw diagonal lines across the fabric, 1⅜ inches (3.5 cm) apart. Cut all of the strips.

2. Put every two strips together with right sides facing at right angles. Mark the seam line and then sew them all together. (Tip: For stretch fabrics, such as cotton interlock, it is easier to make binding tape along the crosswise grain.)

3. Use a plain seam finish for the seam allowances. Trim the opposite corners off.

Bound finish for a straight seam

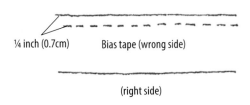

¼ inch (0.7cm) Bias tape (wrong side)

(right side)

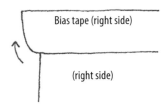

Bias tape (right side)

(right side)

1. Align one edge of the bias tape and the fabric together with right sides facing and then sew them together.

2. Press the bias tape away from the main fabric, as if to wrap it around the seam allowance.

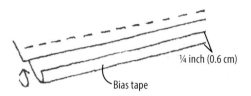

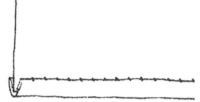

¼ inch (0.6 cm)

Bias tape

3. Fold the raw edge of the bias tape under just enough so that, when folded over, it covers the previous seam.

4. Fold the tape over and then blind stitch the bias tape in place. Be sure the stitches do not show. You can also edge-stitch the tape in place.

Bound finish for a curved seam

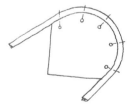

1. Align one edge of the bias tape and the fabric together with right sides facing and pin them in place.

2. Stitch them together along the seam line.

3. Press the bias tape away from the main fabric and then fold under the raw edge of the bias tape inward just enough so that, when folded over, it covers the previous seam.

4. Fold the tape over and then blind-stitch the bias tape in place. Be sure the stitches do not show. You can also sew it in place with an edge stitch on the right side of the fabric.

Making fabric straps
Folding method

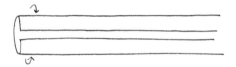

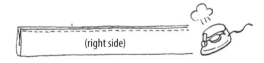

(right side)

1. Fold both sides of the fabric strip to the center with wrong sides together and press.

2. Fold the strip in half with wrong sides together. Iron it flat and then edge-stitch along the folded edges.

Turning method

(wrong side)

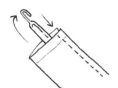

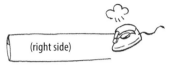

(right side)

1. Fold the fabric strip in half with right sides facing and sew.

2. Turn the strip right side out with a loop turner.

3. After turning the strip right side out, iron the strip and then edge-stitch both sides.

Making decorative fabric-covered buttons

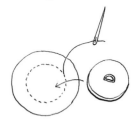

1. Cut a round piece of the fabric large enough to cover the entire button completely. Sew a running stitch along the inner edge of the fabric. Don't cut the thread after stitching.

2. Put the button in the middle of the stitched fabric piece. Pull the ends of the thread until the fabric gathers up and wraps around the button.

3. Carefully clean up the back side of the button.

Gathering fabric
By hand

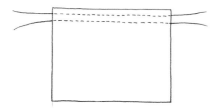 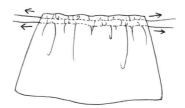

1. Sew two running stitch seams along the edge, leaving a 4–6-inch (10–15-cm) thread tail at both ends.

2. Match up the center of your fabric with your main project and then pull the threads to gather the fabric toward the middle. Make slight adjustments so the fabric is the size you need.

By machine

You can gather fabric by machine by lengthening your machine stitch or by using a gathering foot directly on the fabric edge.

Basic knitting and crocheting

The needleworking projects introduced in this book only require basic knitting and crocheting skills. By making yourself familiar with these basics, you can easily complete those projects.

Gauge swatch

Knitting or crocheting a small sample can show the number of stitches and rows in a 4- x 4- inch (10- x 10-cm) area. The gauge needed varies from pattern to pattern, and the resulting gauge can depend on the size of the yarn and needles.

- Before knitting/crocheting your project, make a 6- x 6-inch (15- x 15-cm) square with your yarn and crochet hook or knitting needles.

- Spread the piece flat with your palms and then iron.

- Count the number of stitches and rows in a 4- x 4-inch (10- x 10-cm) area.

- Compare this to the gauge required for your project. Increase or decrease the size of your needles/hook accordingly.

Basic knitting skills

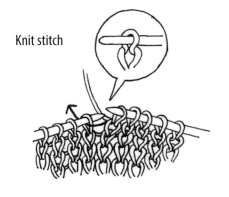

Knit stitch

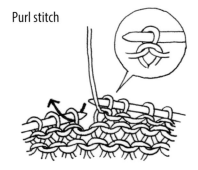

Purl stitch

Basic knitting chart stitches

Stockinette stitch: The most basic knitting pattern. Knit on every right side row and then purl on every wrong side row. It is stretchable.

Knit one, purl one ribbing: Alternating knitting and purling in every other stitch. Mostly used to make up the hems, necks, and cuffs of sweaters.

Reverse stockinette stitch: The back side of stockinette stitch.

Basic crochet stitches

Chain

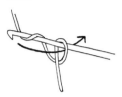

Single crochet

Double crochet

Dog Clothing Tips

What do I need to know when dressing up my dog?

Humans wear clothing to keep warm and to protect their skin. Dogs, however, have hair for those purposes already. Therefore, it is better to put clothes on dogs only when going outside or when it is getting cold. For shaggy dogs, you can comb their hair after taking off the clothing to prevent their hair from getting tangled. If you find your dog has any sort of skin inflammation, you should wait until his skin condition is stable to put clothes on him again.

It is not recommended to put shoes on dogs. It might seem like putting shoes on dogs isn't a problem, but it is similar to putting high heels on humans: although we can walk, it is not comfortable at all.

If you want to tie your dog's hair or tie accessories on their ears and tails, you need to make sure there is nothing abnormal on their skin first. Be careful not to tie things on too tightly—that could cause hair loss.

When putting clothing on their dog for the first time, many owners force their dog's head and four limbs through the holes even when the clothing is too small. Forcing dogs to wear clothes, especially too-small clothes, will not only result in their extreme reluctance to wear clothes in the future, but will also cause too much pressure on their bodies. Even more seriously, it could cause joint discomfort.

After putting clothes on dogs, be sure to check if there are any problems, such as if their arms, legs, armpits, and neck are fitted too tightly, whether they can move freely, and whether there is static electricity shocking them.

How do I take care of my dog's clothing and accessories?

Use the proper detergent for the fabric the clothing is made from, and hand wash instead of machine washing. After washing, wring the clothing gently, dry them in the sun, and then iron them. By following this procedure, you can ensure that the clothing keeps its original shape. If your dog has sensitive skin, you can use a special detergent for babies.

Dog cushions and beds must be cleaned very carefully. Without proper cleaning and maintenance, they could negatively affect your dog's health. Therefore, it is very important to take the time to clean them properly. You can use a vacuum cleaner to clean up the hairs on cushions or beds every day. You should always be sure to vacuum up any hair before washing pet bedding. After washing, hang the pieces in the shade to dry in the open air. Adjust the shape of bedding while hanging it. By following this procedure, you can lengthen the life of your pet's bedding.

Projects

Part 2

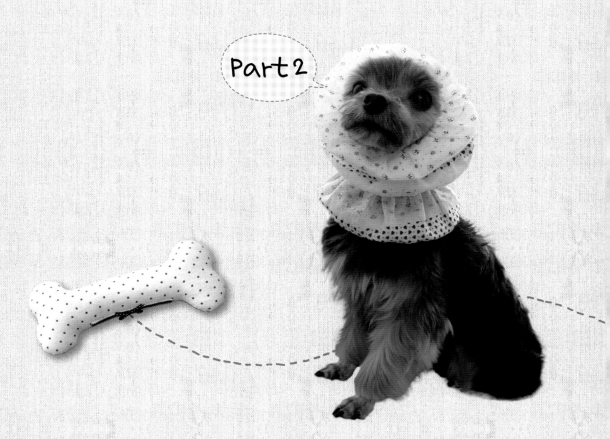

Happy times with my puppy

Fish Toys

Curious puppies will enjoy these plush pull toys. You can engage your pup in an interactive game—as you pull the string, he will respond to the toy's movement and sound. We suggest using organic fabric that will be safe for your puppy. Be careful that the wooden eyes, rattles, and pom-poms do not detach from the toy, as these are choking hazards.

How to MAKE

Fish Toys

FINISHED SIZE large fish, 7⅞ inches x 2½ inches (20 x 6.5 cm); small fish, 5½ inches x 1⅞ inches (14 x 4.6 cm); mini fish (make two), 2¼ inches x 1⅜ inches (5.7 x 3.5 cm)

FABRIC ⅛ yard (⅛ m) striped organic terrycloth in blue
⅛ yard (⅛ m) striped organic terrycloth in brown

NOTIONS Twelve multicolored pom-poms (six for each fish)
Cotton string: ⅔ yard (⅔ m) for large fish; ½ yard (½ m) for small fish
Batting
Four wooden buttons
Two small rattles
Fishing line

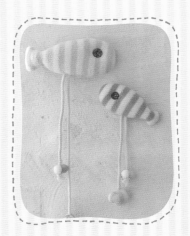

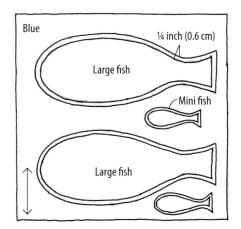

Blue   ¼ inch (0.6 cm)

Large fish

Mini fish

Large fish

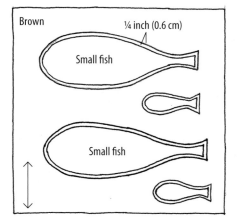

Brown   ¼ inch (0.6 cm)

Small fish

Small fish

1. **Cut the fabric pattern pieces out.** Lay the pattern pieces on the wrong side of the fabric and trace the pattern. Add a ¼-inch (0.6-cm) seam allowance around all sides and then cut out the fabric pieces.

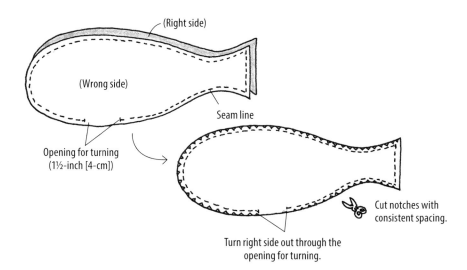

(Right side)

(Wrong side)

Seam line

Opening for turning
(1½-inch [4-cm])

Cut notches with
consistent spacing.

Turn right side out through the
opening for turning.

2. **Sew the large and small fish.** Follow the same instructions for the large fish and small fish toys: Align the raw edges of the fabric together with right sides facing and then sew around the edges, leaving the 1½-inch (4-cm) opening for turning. Press the seam and then cut consistent notches in the seam allowance at the curves. Turn the fish right side out.

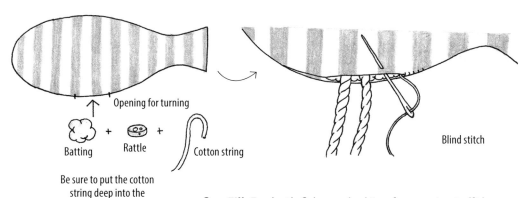

Opening for turning

Batting + Rattle + Cotton string

Be sure to put the cotton
string deep into the
opening.

Blind stitch

3. **Fill.** For both fish, use locking forceps to stuff the batting into the opening. Fold the cotton string in half and insert the folded end, along with the rattle, into the opening. Note that the two ends of the cotton string do not need to be the same length. Close up the opening with blind stitches to finish.

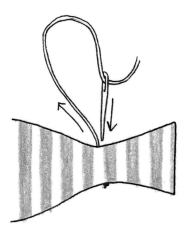

4. **Add the eyes and adjust the shape.** Sew the wooden buttons onto each fish for the eyes. Stitch vertically through the top and bottom of the base of each tail to make them look puffier.

5. **Make and connect the two mini fish.** Sew the mini fish the same way as the larger fish. Secure one end of the cotton string from the large fish into the opening of one of the mini fish and close it up with blind stitches; do the same for the small fish and the other mini fish. Tie a knot at each remaining end of cotton string and attach the pom-poms with fishing line.

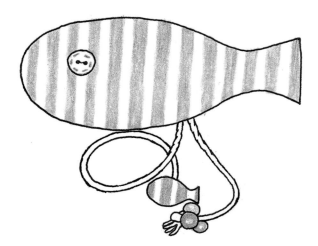

Plush Bone

This bone-shaped toy will be one of your dog's favorites. Give him the toy, and watch his tail start wagging! Supervise your dog with this toy and do not allow him to remove the bell from the center.

 This soft toy is a good size for most small and medium-sized dogs.

How to Make

Plush Bone

FINISHED SIZE	9⅝ inches x 4⅜ inches (24.5 x 11 cm)
FABRIC	¼ yard (¼ m) polka-dot linen
NOTIONS	4¾ inches (12 cm) ⅜-inch- (1-cm-) wide ribbon Decorative bow Batting Small bell

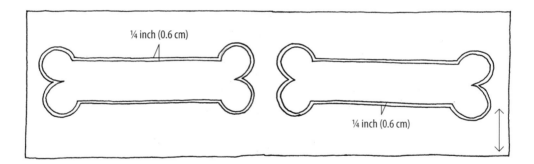

¼ inch (0.6 cm)

¼ inch (0.6 cm)

1. **Cut the fabric pattern pieces out.** Lay the pattern pieces on the wrong side of the fabric and trace the pattern. Add a ¼-inch (0.6-cm) seam allowance around all edges and then cut out the fabric pieces.

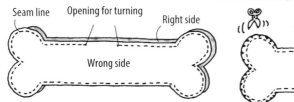

Seam line   Opening for turning

Right side

Wrong side

Cut notches at curves and corners.

Turn right side out through the opening for turning.

Wrong side

2. **Sew.** Layer the two linen pieces together with right sides facing and sew around the perimeter, leaving a 2-inch (5-cm) opening for turning as the pattern indicates. Cut notches into the seam allowance at 3⁄8-inch (1-cm) intervals along the corners and curves. Turn the bone right side out through the opening.

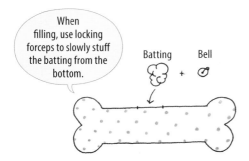

When filling, use locking forceps to slowly stuff the batting from the bottom.

Batting   Bell

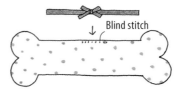

Blind stitch

3. **Fill and insert the bell.** Fill the bone carefully through the opening and insert the bell into the center of the filling.

4. **Close the opening and add the bow.** Close up the opening with blind stitches. Stitch on the ribbon at the position of the opening with blind or overcast stitches and then stitch the bow onto the center of the ribbon.

Cute Dog Snood

When your dog is eating or drinking, the snood protects the ears and ear hair from getting dirty. Use a soft and lightweight cotton fabric that will be comfortable for your dog to wear.

How to Make Cute Dog Snood

FINISHED SIZE	S, M, L
FABRIC	½ yard (½ m) light cotton fabric
NOTIONS	14 inches (35 cm) ⅛-inch- (0.4-cm-) wide decorative lace
	1½–2¼ yards (1½–2¼ m) of ¼-inch- (0.6-cm-) wide elastic
	Bodkin or safety pin for threading the elastic

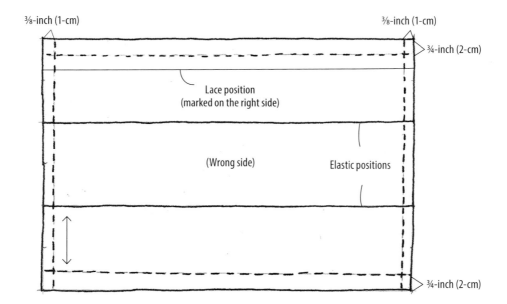

⅜-inch (1-cm) ⅜-inch (1-cm)

¾-inch (2-cm)

Lace position
(marked on the right side)

(Wrong side)   Elastic positions

¾-inch (2-cm)

1. **Cut out the fabric pattern pieces.** Lay the pattern pieces on the wrong side of the fabric and trace the pattern. You'll be using a ¾-inch (2-cm) seam allowance on the top and bottom edges and a ⅜-inch (1-cm) seam allowance on the left and right. This is already marked on the paper pattern. Mark the positions of the lace and elastic on the fabric.

2. **Sew the lace in place.** Line up the lace along the marked pattern guideline on the right side of the fabric and then edge-stitch it in place.

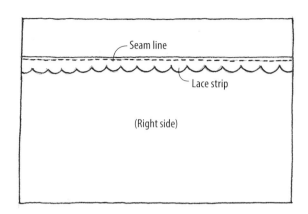

Seam line

Lace strip

(Right side)

Backstitch several times at both ends. Stretch the elastic slightly while sewing.

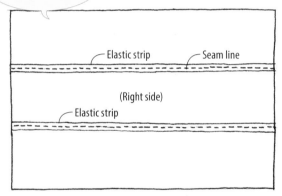

Elastic strip   Seam line

(Right side)

Elastic strip

3. **Sew the elastic in place.** Cut the elastic strips slightly longer than your dog's neck circumference and then align them along the marked pattern guidelines on the wrong side of the fabric. Using a long stitch length, sew the elastic in place while slightly stretching it.

4. **Sew the snood, step 1.** Fold the fabric in half widthwise with right sides facing and sew it along the edge. Overlock the seam allowance or fold it under by ¼ inch (0.6 cm) twice and sew it in place.

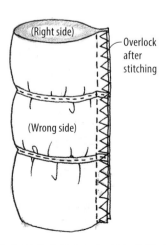

(Right side)

Overlock after stitching

(Wrong side)

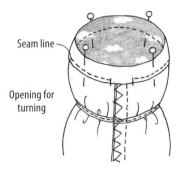

Seam line

Opening for turning

5. **Sew the snood, step 2.** Fold the top edge of the collar under by ⅜ inch (1 cm) twice and then pin the fold in place. Stitch it in place, close to the fold, and be sure to leave a small hole for inserting more elastic (the smaller, the better) somewhere near the side seam allowance.

6. **Cut and insert the elastic strip.** Cut your elastic strips based on your measurements from the sidebar below. Insert the first elastic strip into the upper casing with a bodkin or safety pin. When you've gotten one end all the way through, overlap it with the previous end and sew them together. Sew up the opening that you made previously for the elastic. Repeat steps 5 and 6 for the bottom edge of the snood.

insert the elastic

Calculate the length of the elastic needed. Measure the circumference of your dog's head with the tape going vertically. The length of the elastic should be ¾–2 inches (2–5cm) shorter than the head circumference plus ⅜ inch (1 cm) seam allowance at each end. For example, if your dog's head circumference is 9⅞ inches (25 cm), you will need to cut two elastic strips at 9⅞ – 1⅛ + ¾ inches = 9½ inches (25 – 3 + 2 cm = 24 cm). If you are making a large snood, you should use thicker elastic strips.

Head circumference (vertical)

Heart Pattern Place Mat

Dogs can be messy when they eat and drink, spilling food and water on the floor around their bowls. A cute, washable place mat not only looks nice but also makes mealtime cleaner.

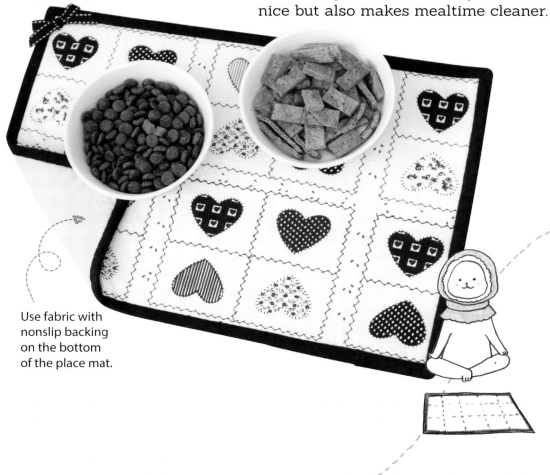

Use fabric with nonslip backing on the bottom of the place mat.

Heart Pattern Place Mat

FINISHED SIZE 15¾ inches x 10 ¼ inches (40 x 26 cm)

FABRIC ½ yard (½ m) of 100 percent cotton with heart pattern

NOTIONS ½ yard (½ m) of fusible fleece interfacing
½ yard (½ m) of nonslip fabric
1⅔ yards (1⅔ m) of linen bias tape
Decorative bow

Heart patterned cotton (wrong side)

Nonslip fabric (wrong side)

Fusible fleece

1. **Cut out the fabric pattern pieces.** Trace a 15¾ x 10 ¼-inch (40 x 26-cm) rectangle on the wrong side of the cotton, fusible fleece, and nonslip fabric. Cut out all of the fabric pieces, allowing an extra 1–2 inches (2.5–5 cm) around the fusible fleece and nonslip fabric.

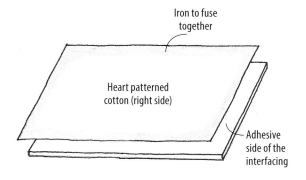

Iron to fuse together

Heart patterned cotton (right side)

Adhesive side of the interfacing

2. **Iron the fusible fleece.** Align the wrong side of the patterned cotton to the adhesive side of the fusible fleece. From the right side of the patterned cotton, iron to fuse the two fabrics.

3. **Baste in place.** Layer the nonslip fabric beneath the fusible fleece and baste all three layers together. The order should be nonslip fabric (wrong side up), fusible fleece, patterned cotton (right side up).

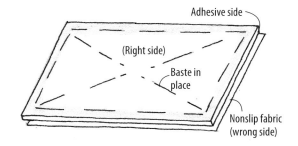

Adhesive side

(Right side)

Baste in place

Nonslip fabric (wrong side)

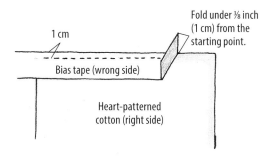

Fold under ⅜ inch (1 cm) from the starting point.

1 cm

Bias tape (wrong side)

Heart-patterned cotton (right side)

4. **Start the binding.** To bind the four edges of the fabric, begin by aligning the raw edge of the bias tape with the mat, right sides facing. Fold in the first ⅜ inch (1 cm) of the tape and start stitching it in place with a ⅜-inch (1-cm) seam allowance.

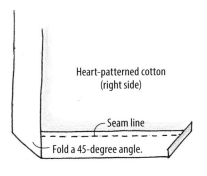

Heart-patterned cotton
(right side)

Seam line

Fold a 45-degree angle.

5. **Binding, part 1.** Continue stitching down the side with a ⅜-inch (1-cm) seam allowance. When you reach the corner, make a diagonal fold.

6. **Binding, part 2.** Begin stitching the next edge, starting from the corner and not sewing over the fold that you just made. Continue with the other three corners until you reach the end. Overlap the finishing end of the tape with the starting end. Sew the two ends together and then press the seam open.

Don't stitch across the right-angle fold.

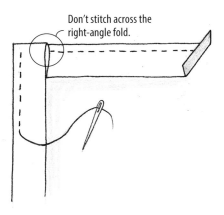

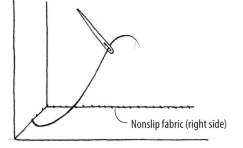

Nonslip fabric (right side)

7. **Wrap up.** Fold the bias tape around the seam allowance and press it toward the nonslip fabric. Fold under the raw edge and blind-stitch it in place along the wrong side of the mat. To finish, stitch the decorative bow to one corner of the mat.

Let's play with toys!

Ball

This ball toy is suitable for young puppies and small dogs. You throw the ball for your pup to fetch and play similar games with him. The ball is not meant to be a chew toy because the button decorations and rattle inside are choking hazards.

Ball

FINISHED SIZE	2 inches (5 cm) in diameter
FABRIC	¼-yard (¼ m) or 7 x 5-inch (16 x 12-cm) scrap of ivory linen
	¼-yard (¼ m) or 7 x 5-inch (16 x 12-cm) scrap of polka-dot linen
NOTIONS	Green and yellow embroidery floss
	Cotton batting
	Small rattle
	Two wooden buttons

Ivory linen

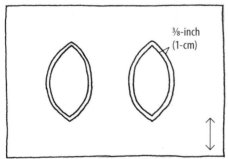

Polka-dot linen

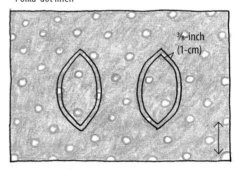

1. **Cut out the fabric pattern pieces .** Lay the pattern pieces on the wrong side of the fabric and trace the pattern. Add a ⅜-inch (1-cm) seam allowance and then cut out the fabric pieces: two pieces of ivory linen and two pieces of polka-dot linen.

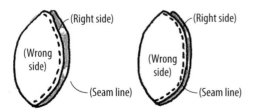

2. **Join the fabric pieces, part 1.** Align one ivory linen piece and one polka-dot linen piece together with right sides facing. Align the top points and the center curve and then stitch the pieces together along one curved edge. Repeat this with the remaining pair of fabric pieces.

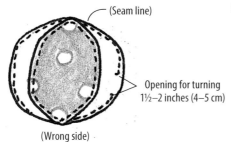

(Seam line)

Opening for turning
1½–2 inches (4–5 cm)

(Wrong side)

3. **Join the fabric pieces, part 2.** Align the two pairs of linen pieces from step 2 and sew them together around the perimeter, leaving a 1½–2 inch (4–5 cm) opening (depending on the size of the rattle) for turning.

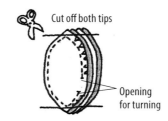

Cut off both tips

Opening for turning

4. **Trim the seam allowance.** Trim the seam allowances to ¼ inch (0.5 cm) and trim the top and bottom corners of excess fabric.

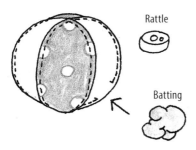

Rattle

Batting

5. **Fill and put in the rattle.** Turn the ball right side out through the opening for turning. Stuff it with batting and then place the rattle into the center. Start to sew it closed with blind stitches, but keep filling it slowly with small pieces of batting for a nice, round shape until you make your last stitch.

6. **Add decorative stitches.** Using the embroidery floss, sew a running stitch along the ivory linen, just inside the seams. To finish, attach the wooden buttons on the top and bottom center points of the ball. Caution: When a dog holds this ball in his mouth, it is easy for him to get the threads stuck in his teeth. We recommend sewing this project by hand with the smallest stitches you can manage.

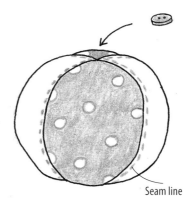

Seam line

Flying Disc

Puppies who like to play will enjoy this small flying disc. This fabric toy will withstand a little bit of chewing, as long as your dog cannot remove the rattle inside, but it is more suitable for throwing and fetching games.

HOW TO MAKE

Flying Disc

FINISHED SIZE	6 inches (15 cm) in diameter
FABRIC	¼ yard (¼ m) ivory linen
	⅛ yard (⅛ m) polka-dot linen
NOTIONS	Embroidery floss
	Cotton batting
	Small rattle

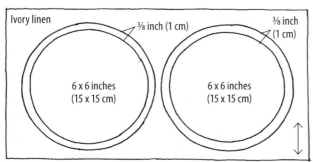

Ivory linen ⅜ inch (1 cm) ⅜ inch (1 cm)

6 x 6 inches (15 x 15 cm)

6 x 6 inches (15 x 15 cm)

Polka-dot linen

3⅛ x 3⅛ inches (8 x 8 cm)

1. **Cut the fabric pattern pieces out.** Lay the pattern pieces on the wrong side of the fabric and trace the pattern. Add a ⅜-inch (1-cm) seam allowance for the two ivory pieces but not for the polka-dot linen piece. Cut out the fabric pieces.

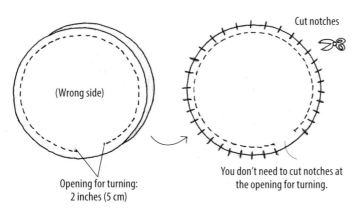

(Wrong side)

Opening for turning: 2 inches (5 cm)

Cut notches

You don't need to cut notches at the opening for turning.

2. **Sew the large disc.** Layer the two large 6- x 6-inch (15- x 15-cm) discs together with right sides facing. Sew around the perimeter, remembering to leave a 2-inch (5-cm) opening for turning. After sewing, cut notches in the seam allowance at ⅜-inch (1-cm) intervals around the edge.

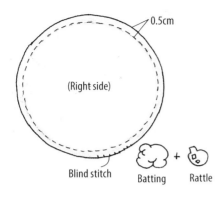

0.5cm

(Right side)

Blind stitch   Batting   Rattle

3. **Fill and put in the rattle.** Stuff the batting through the opening and insert the rattle at the center of the filling. Close the opening with blind stitches. Sew a running stitch around the perimeter of the disc with embroidery floss ¼ inch (0.6 cm) from the previous seam.

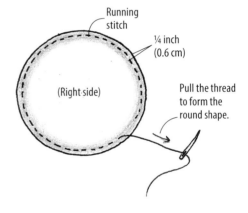

Running stitch

¼ inch (0.6 cm)

(Right side)

Pull the thread to form the round shape.

4. **Sew the small disc.** Draw a smaller circle within the polka-dot linen circle ¼ inch (0.6 cm) in from the edge. Stitch along this line with a hand-sewn running stitch and then pull the thread so that the edges tuck under in a uniform circle shape.

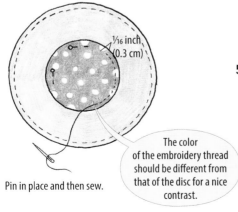

1/16 inch (0.3 cm)

The color of the embroidery thread should be different from that of the disc for a nice contrast.

Pin in place and then sew.

5. **Attach the two discs.** Align the small disc in the center of the large disc and pin it in place. Shift the rattle in the batting to the center if needed. Sew a running stitch 1/16 inch (0.3 cm) in from the edge around the perimeter of the small disc with embroidery floss.

Toy Storage Basket

Put your dog's toys in a pretty storage basket to match your décor. Place it where he can grab his favorites anytime he wants to play.

How to Make
Toy Storage Basket

FINISHED SIZE | 13 inches (33 cm) in diameter; 4 ⅜ inches (11cm) in height

FABRIC | ⅔ yard (⅔ m) cotton patchwork fabric
⅔ yard (⅔ m) linen fabric (for lining)

NOTIONS | 11½ x 11½-inch (29 x 29-cm) square plastic or cardboard
Cotton batting
2 yards (2 m) decorative lace

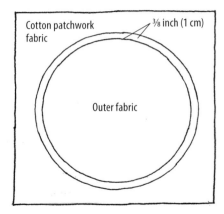

Cotton patchwork fabric

⅜ inch (1 cm)

Outer fabric

1. **Cut out the fabric pattern pieces.** Lay the pattern pieces on the wrong side of the outer fabric and the right side of the lining fabric and then trace the patterns. Add a ⅜-inch (1-cm) seam allowance for all pieces and cut them out. Mark the cross lines between the inner and outer circles on the lining fabric.

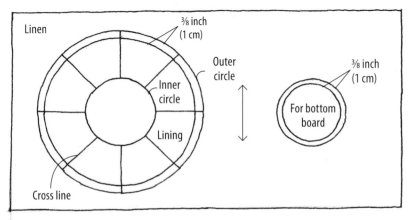

Linen

⅜ inch (1 cm)

Outer circle

⅜ inch (1 cm)

Inner circle

Lining

For bottom board

Cross line

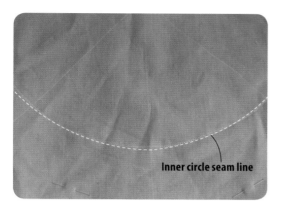

Inner circle seam line

Lining (right side)

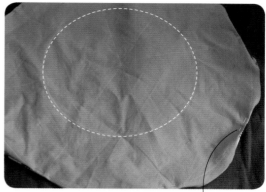

Fold in ⅜ inch (1 cm) and pin in place.

2. **Stitch the inner circle.** Layer the outer fabric and lining together with wrong sides facing and pin them in place. Stitch along the inner circle as marked on the lining (and the paper pattern). Fold under ⅜ inch (1 cm) along the edge of the outer fabric and the lining around the outer circle and then pin the folds in place.

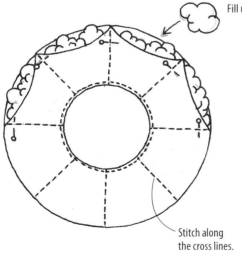

Fill until ⅔ full.

Stitch along the cross lines.

3. **Stitch the cross lines.** Stitch along the cross lines marked on the lining starting from the inner circle out to the outer circle. Fill the slots ⅔ full with batting. Pin together the folded edges of the outer circle lining and outer fabric.

4. **Make ruffles.** Sew a running stitch around the perimeter of the outer circle ¼ inch (0.6 cm) inside the outer edge with even ¼-inch (0.6-cm) stitches. Pull the thread as you sew to create even gathers.

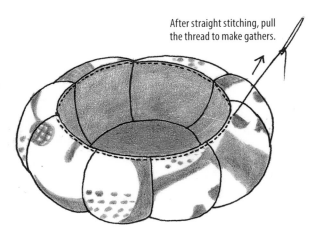

After straight stitching, pull the thread to make gathers.

5. **Add the lace trim on the hem.** Gather the lace trim until it is short enough to cover the running seam and then sew the lace along the gathered edge.

6. **Adjust the shape.** For the bottom board fabric, sew a running stitch ¼ inch (0.6 cm) in from the edge around the perimeter. Check to be sure the board fits securely in the bottom of the basket. If it does, put the board in the center of the fabric and pull the threads to cinch it up around the board. Tie a knot to finish.

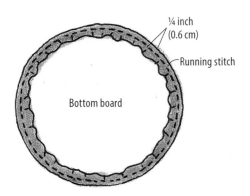

¼ inch
(0.6 cm)

Running stitch

Bottom board

7. **Insert the bottom board.** Put the bottom board made in step 6 into the basket to finish.

There are two kinds of plastic boards for bag bottoms: hard and soft. The soft board is recommended for this project because it strong yet soft enough to cut with scissors. You can use cardboard instead of a plastic board.

Pillow Set

When your dog is ready to relax, he will appreciate having his own pillow on which he can lie down. I recommend using a soft, warm microfiber fabric to keep him comfortable. This set also includes matching smaller round and heart-shaped pillows on which he can rest his head.

 Consider your dog's size and adjust the measurements of the pillow set if necessary.

Pillow Set

Large Pillow

FINISHED SIZE	29 1/8 x 22 1/2 inches (74 x 57 cm)
FABRIC	1 1/3 yards (1 1/3 m) blue padded microfiber fabric
NOTIONS	3 yards (3 m) decorative lace Cotton batting Five buttons Basting thread

Round and Heart-Shaped Pillows

FINISHED SIZE	heart-shaped pillow 9 5/8 x 8 7/8" inches (24.5 x 22.5 cm); round pillow 10 x 10 inches (25.5 x 25.5 cm)
FABRIC	1/3 yard (1/3 m) blue padded microfiber fabric
NOTIONS	2 yards (2 m) decorative lace (1 yard [1 m] for each pillow) cotton batting One button One decorative bow Basting thread

Making the large pillow

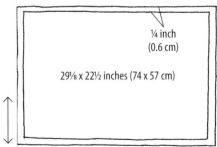

1/4 inch (0.6 cm)

29 1/8 x 22 1/2 inches (74 x 57 cm)

1/4 inch (0.6 cm)

29 1/8 x 22 1/2 inches (74 x 57 cm)

1. **Cut the fabric pattern pieces out.** Trace two 29 1/8 x 22 1/2-inch (74 x 57-cm) rectangles on the wrong side of the fabric. Add a 1/4-inch (0.6 cm) seam allowance around all the edges and cut the fabric pieces out.

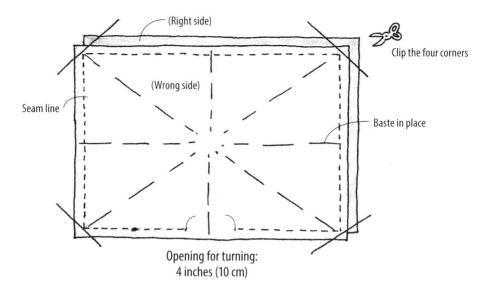

(Right side)

(Wrong side)

Seam line

Clip the four corners

Baste in place

Opening for turning:
4 inches (10 cm)

2. **Sew.** Layer the two pillow pieces with right sides facing and baste the layers together to secure their position before sewing. Sew them together around the perimeter but leave a 4–6-inch (10–15-cm) opening for turning. Clip the corners of the seam allowances.

3. **Attach the lace trim.** Turn the cushion right side out through the opening. Sew the lace around the finished seam, starting from the opening (leave enough extra lace at the beginning to cover the opening) and going around the perimeter. When you reach the end, fold under the finishing end of the lace and overlap it over the starting end. Fill the pillow with batting, starting at the bottom and filling gradually.

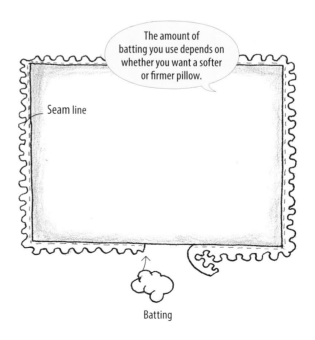

The amount of batting you use depends on whether you want a softer or firmer pillow.

Seam line

Batting

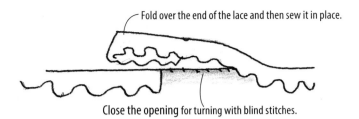

Fold over the end of the lace and then sew it in place.

Close the opening for turning with blind stitches.

4. **Close the opening for turning.** Close the opening for turning with blind stitches. Fold under ⅜–¾ inch (1–2 cm) of the lace at the beginning end and overlap the two ends before sewing them to the edge.

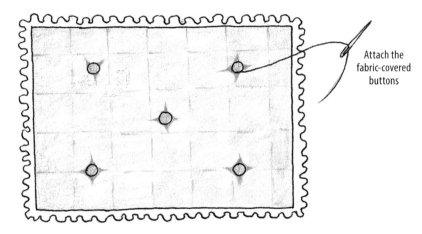

Attach the fabric-covered buttons

5. **Make and attach the fabric-covered buttons.** Cover five buttons with the same fabric used for the pillow. Use a long, thick needle to hand-stitch the buttons, spaced evenly, across the top of pillow as in the illustration. Pull the thread taut to achieve a puffy look. After the buttons are securely attached, readjust the batting as needed.

Optional: To keep the pillow from sliding on the floor, you can add a piece of nonslip fabric on the bottom. In our example, the top of the cushion is made of microfiber fabric and the bottom is a combination of microfiber and nonslip fabric.

Making the round and heart-shaped pillows

(steps 1–4 are the same for both pillows)

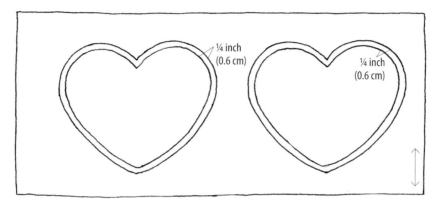

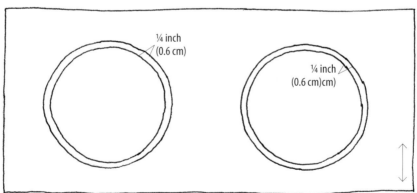

1. **Cut out the fabric pattern pieces .** Lay the pattern pieces on the wrong side of the fabric and trace the patterns. Add a ¼-inch (0.6-cm) seam allowance and cut out the fabric pieces.

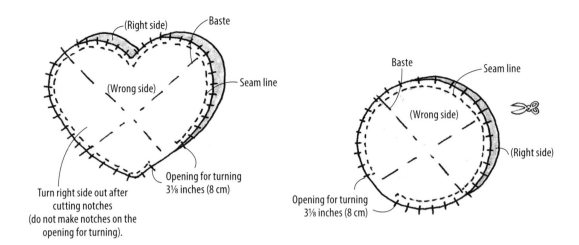

(Right side) Baste

(Wrong side)

Seam line

Turn right side out after
cutting notches
(do not make notches on the
opening for turning).

Opening for turning
3⅛ inches (8 cm)

Baste

Seam line

(Wrong side)

(Right side)

Opening for turning
3⅛ inches (8 cm)

2. **Baste.** Align the fabric pieces together with right sides facing and baste them with basting thread to secure the pieces for stitching. Sew around the perimeter, leaving a 3⅛-inch (8-cm) opening for turning. Cut notches along the seam-allowance curves at equal spacing. Turn the pillow right side out through the opening.

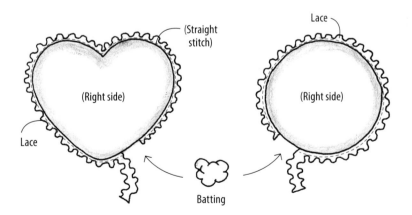

(Straight
stitch)

Lace

(Right side)

(Right side)

Lace

Lace

Batting

3. **Attach the lace trim.** Start to sew the lace around the previous seam. Begin just outside the opening, leaving enough lace to cover the opening, and then start sewing the lace in place. When you reach the end, reserve enough lace to fold over one edge and overlap it with the beginning. Fill the pillow to your desired firmness, making sure to add the batting uniformly for the best shape.

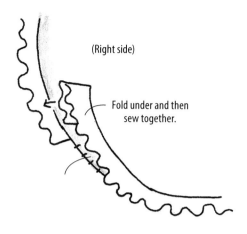

(Right side)

Fold under and then sew together.

4. **Close the opening for turning.** Close the opening for turning with blind stitches. Fold under ⅜–¾ inch (1–2cm) at the end of the lace, overlap it with the beginning, and then sew the lace into place.

5. **Sew on the decorations.** Sew the decorative bow onto the heart-shaped pillow. Make a fabric-covered button with the same fabric that you used for the pillows. Use a long, thick needle to hand-stitch the button to the center of the pillow. Pull the thread taut to achieve a puffy look. Secure the button firmly.

Attach the bow.

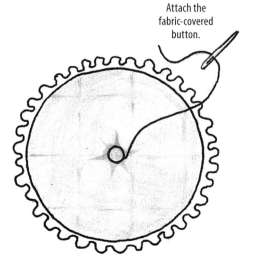

Attach the fabric-covered button.

A Stylish Twist

Belly Band

For a male puppy who is still learning the house-training routine or a male dog who may be "accident" prone, a belly band prevents him from making a mess indoors. This version is made with stylish fabric and is easy for the dog to wear.

Velcro makes the belly band easy to put on and take off.

Made of cotton fabric, the belly band won't irritate the dog's skin.

Belly Band

SIZES	XS–XL
FABRIC	⅛ yard (⅛ m) polka-dot cotton for outer fabric ⅛ yard (⅛ m) 100 percent cotton terrycloth for lining
NOTIONS	1–1⅓ yard (1–1⅓ m) thin decorative lace 3½ inches (9 cm) 1-inch- (2.5-cm-) wide Velcro ⅛ yard (⅛ m) lightweight fusible interfacing

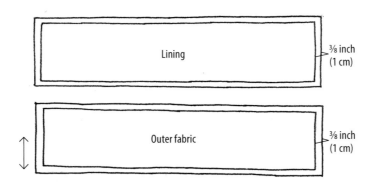

1. **Cut out the fabric pattern pieces.** Lay the pattern pieces on the wrong side of the fabric and trace the pattern. Add a ⅜-inch(1 cm) seam allowance around all sides and then cut out the fabric pieces. Cut out one additional band piece from the interfacing.

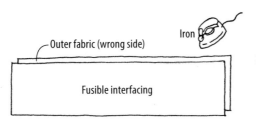

2. **Iron the fusible interfacing.** Lay the fusible interfacing on the wrong side of the outer fabric and then iron to fuse it in place.

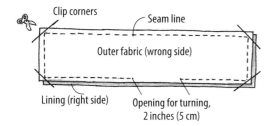

Clip corners
Seam line
Outer fabric (wrong side)
Lining (right side)
Opening for turning,
2 inches (5 cm)

3. **Sew the outer fabric and lining together.** Align the outer fabric and lining pieces together with right sides facing and sew them together around the perimeter, leaving a 2-inch (5-cm) opening for turning. Trim the seam allowances to ¼ inch (0.6 cm) and clip the corners.

Adjust the corners and edges and then press flat.

Sew the lace in place.

4. **Turn right side out through the opening for turning.** Turn the band right side out through the opening and then carefully pick the corners out into shape with a needle. Iron the piece flat and then close up the opening with blind stitches.

5. **Sew the lace in place.** Align the lace around the perimeter of the band and then sew it in place along the four edges. Pivot the lace at the corners. When you reach the starting point, fold the end of the lace under and overlap it over the beginning before stitching in place.

6. **Attach the Velcro.** Stitch the hook side of the Velcro onto the left of the band from the right side. Stitch the loop side of the Velcro onto the right side of the lining part of the band. You can stitch the Velcro on with a machine or by hand, whichever you prefer.

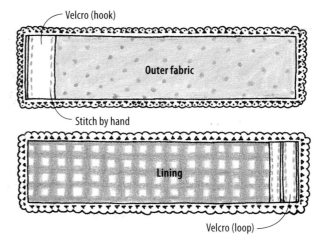

Velcro (hook)
Outer fabric
Stitch by hand
Lining
Velcro (loop)

Special Dog Steps

When dogs, especially young puppies and senior dogs, jump on and off of furniture, they can damage their joints. Stairs can help your dog climb up and down without causing joint problems. Make these simple steps and teach your dog to use them.

Using the steps is easy!

Special Dog Steps

FINISHED SIZE   small, 19⅝ x 7⅞ x 6⅜ inches (50 x 20 x 16 cm); large, 19⅝ x 27½ x 6⅜ inches (50 x 70 x 16 cm)

FABRIC   ¼–⅔ yard (¼–⅔ m) cotton/linen blend for top
¼–⅔ yard (¼–⅔ m) striped linen for sides
1¼–2 yards (1¼–2m) waterproof fabric for lining
¼–⅔ yard (¼–⅔ m) nonslip fabric for bottom

NOTIONS   19⅝ x 7⅞ x 6⅜ inches (50 x 20 x 16 cm) visco-elastic memory foam (small)
40-inch zipper (small)
19⅝ x 27½ x 6⅜ inches (50 x 70 x 16 cm) visco-elastic memory foam (large)
63-inch zipper (large)
2 yards (2 m) ⅜-inch- (1-cm-) wide elastic

1. **Cut out the fabric pieces.** Cut out the required rectangles for each fabric; the seam allowances are already included. Cut the foam according to the illustration guide. With the cotton/linen blend, you don't have to cut out the pattern grain; just align the pattern against the stripes in the fabric design.

Note: The same instructions apply for both the large and small steps.

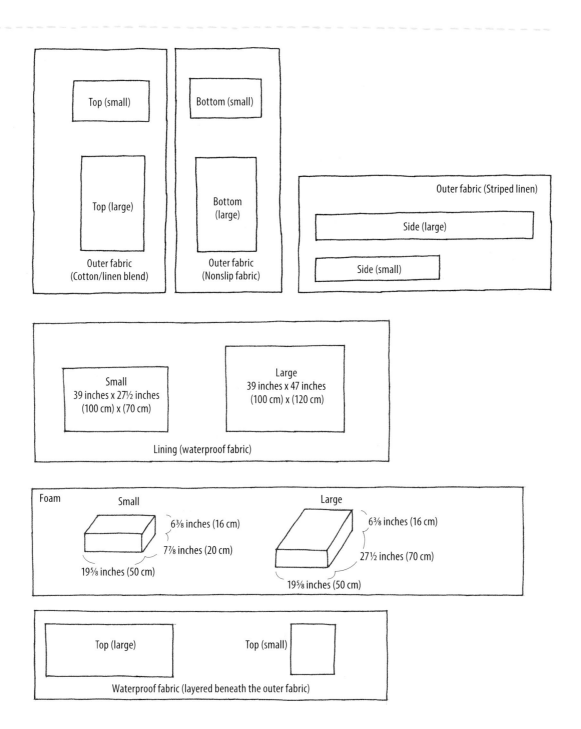

Top (small)

Bottom (small)

Outer fabric (Striped linen)

Top (large)

Bottom (large)

Side (large)

Side (small)

Outer fabric (Cotton/linen blend)

Outer fabric (Nonslip fabric)

Small
39 inches x 27½ inches
(100 cm) x (70 cm)

Large
39 inches x 47 inches
(100 cm) x (120 cm)

Lining (waterproof fabric)

Foam

Small

Large

6⅜ inches (16 cm)

7⅞ inches (20 cm)

19⅝ inches (50 cm)

6⅜ inches (16 cm)

27½ inches (70 cm)

19⅝ inches (50 cm)

Top (large)

Top (small)

Waterproof fabric (layered beneath the outer fabric)

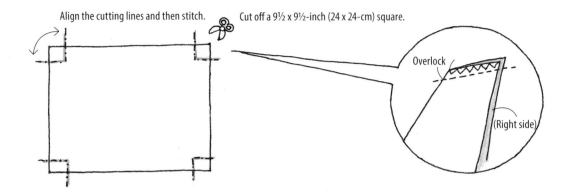

Align the cutting lines and then stitch.

Cut off a 9½ x 9½-inch (24 x 24-cm) square.

Overlock

(Right side)

2. **Make the lining, part 1: Sew.** On the lining piece, cut off 9½ x 9½-inch (24 x 24-cm) squares at the four corners. Fold the fabric diagonally to match up the cut edges with right sides together and then stitch the edges together with a ⅜-inch (1-cm) seam allowance. Overlock the seam allowances when finished.

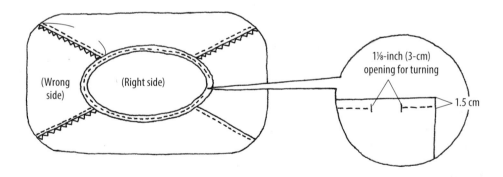

(Wrong side)

(Right side)

1⅛-inch (3-cm) opening for turning

1.5 cm

3. **Make the lining, part 2: Make room for inserting the elastic.** To create the elastic casing, fold under the edge of the lining by ¼ inch (0.6 cm) and then 5/8 inch (1.5 cm). Stitch the fold in place, leaving a 11/8-inch (3-cm) opening for inserting the elastic.

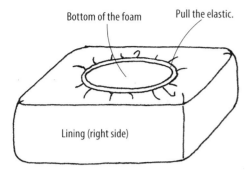

Bottom of the foam

Pull the elastic.

Lining (right side)

4. **Make the lining, part 3: Insert the elastic.** Insert the elastic through the opening with a safety pin or bodkin needle. Tighten the elastic enough that you know you can still fit the foam brick inside the lining. Tie a knot in the elastic and then embed it in the casing.

5. **Assemble the outer fabric, part 1: Add a layer of waterproof fabric.** Layer the step's top outer fabric with the waterproof fabric with wrong sides together and then sew them together around the perimeter. With this layer of waterproof fabric, it will be easy to clean up if your dog soils the step.

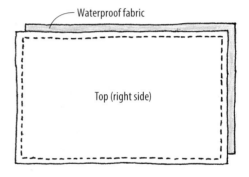

Waterproof fabric

Top (right side)

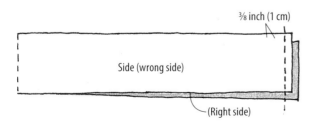

⅜ inch (1 cm)

Side (wrong side)

(Right side)

6. **Assemble the outer fabric, part 2: Make the side.** Fold the striped linen fabric for the side in half with the short sides aligned. Sew them together along this edge with a ⅜-inch (1-cm) seam allowance, creating a loop.

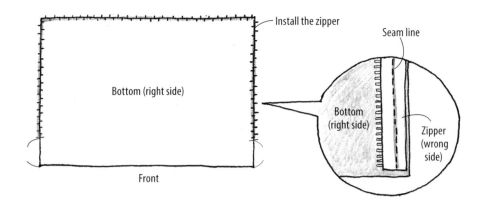

Install the zipper

Seam line

Bottom (right side)

Bottom
(right side)

Zipper
(wrong
side)

Front

7. **Install the zipper, part 1.** Mark two points 7⅞ inches (20 cm) up from the bottom edge of the nonslip fabric. Line up the zipper between these two points, going around the fabric edges as shown in the illustration. Sew the zipper around these edges, stopping short of the marks you made.

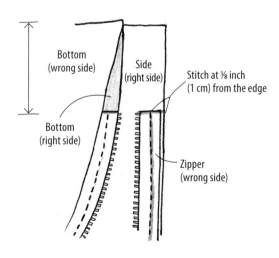

Bottom
(wrong side)

Side
(right side)

Stitch at ⅜ inch
(1 cm) from the edge

Bottom
(right side)

Zipper
(wrong side)

8. **Install the zipper, part 2.** Align the other half of the zipper along the edge of the folded side piece sewn in step 6. Stitch the zipper to the striped linen with right sides facing and a ⅜-inch (1-cm) seam allowance.

9. Join the top and side pieces.
Install the zipper slider if yours was not already attached to the zipper. Align the top piece to the raw edges of the side pieces (without the zipper attached). Make similar 7⅞-inch (20-cm) marks along the bottom edge of the top and make sure that they line up with those on the bottom. Sew around the perimeter of the top.

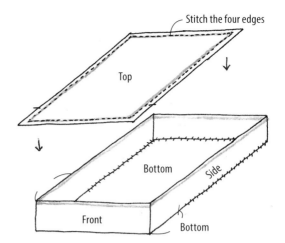

Stitch the four edges

Top

Bottom

Side

Front

Bottom

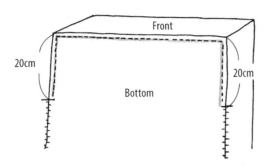

Front

20cm

20cm

Bottom

10. Finishing. Stitch in the gaps left in step 7 along the front and side pieces. To prevent the zipper from falling off, sew several backstitches over the ends of the zipper. To finish, stuff the foam into the lining, slip it into the cover, and zip it up.

Visco-Elastic Foam

When purchasing Visco-Elastic Foam, you can have it cut to the dimensions you desire.

Elizabethan Collar

An Elizabethan collar is essential for preventing dogs from scratching or biting at injuries or wounds. A dog that has surgery is often sent home with an Elizabethan collar so that he won't irritate the surgery site and cause infection. This padded fabric collar is more comfortable than the typical plastic type.

A Velcro closure makes it easy to secure the collar.

This Elizabethan collar is comfortable for a dog to wear.

How to Make Elizabethan Collar

SIZES	XS–XL
FABRIC	¼–½ yard (¼–½-m) patchwork linen
NOTIONS	16" x 8" (40 – 20cm) – 26" x 12" (65 x 30cm) square of foam
	Hook-and-loop or Velcro closure

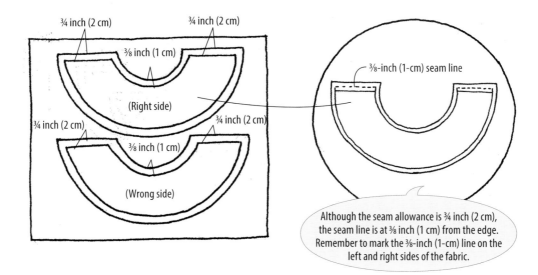

¾ inch (2 cm) ¾ inch (2 cm)

⅜ inch (1 cm)

(Right side)

¾ inch (2 cm) ¾ inch (2 cm)

⅜ inch (1 cm)

(Wrong side)

⅜-inch (1-cm) seam line

Although the seam allowance is ¾ inch (2 cm), the seam line is at ⅜ inch (1 cm) from the edge. Remember to mark the ⅜-inch (1-cm) line on the left and right sides of the fabric.

1. **Cut out the fabric pattern pieces .** Lay the pattern pieces on the wrong side of the fabric and trace the pattern. Add a ⅜-inch (1-cm) seam allowance along the curved edges and a ¾-inch (2-cm) seam allowance along the straight edges (for the hook-and-loop or Velcro). Cut out the fabric pieces. In total, you should have two fabric pieces (outer fabric and lining) and one piece of foam with no seam allowance added. Make sure that the edges of the foam are cut smoothly for the best finished shape.

2. **Sew the collar.** Align the two linen patchwork pieces together with right sides facing and then sew around the perimeter, leaving one straight edge that will serve as the opening for turning. Remember that the seam line is ⅜ inch (1 cm) from the edge.

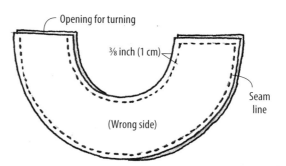

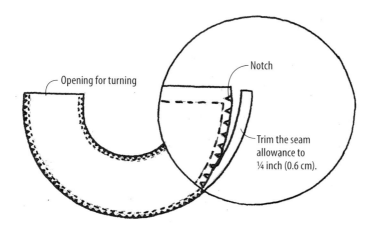

3. **Turn the collar right side out through the opening.** Trim the seam allowance to ¼ inch (0.6 cm). Cut notches along the curved seam allowance spaced ⅜ inch (1 cm) apart. Turn the collar right side out through the opening and flatten out the seams.

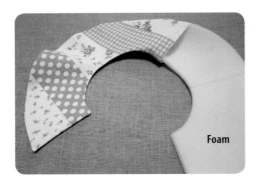 

4. **Insert the foam.** Run a straight seam at the ¾-inch (2-cm) line along the straight edge of the collar. Stuff the foam into the collar from the opening, pushing it as close to the seam line as possible. When complete, the foam should be flush with the ¾-inch (2-cm) seam line marked at the opening edge.

5. **Close the opening for turning, part 1.** Fold under ⅜ inch (1 cm) at the opening, folding it flush with the ⅜-inch (1-cm) marked line. Pin the fold in place and then edge-stitch the folds together.

Stitch the opening edge at the ¾-inch
(2-cm) marked position on the right side.

6. **Close the opening for turning, part 2.** Sew a straight seam along the ¾-inch
    (2-cm) marked line at the opening edge. Push the foam in slightly to prevent
    sewing on it.

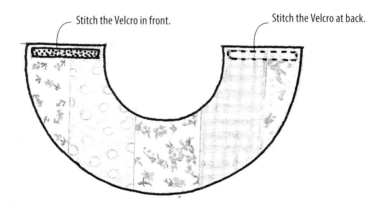

Stitch the Velcro in front.   Stitch the Velcro at back.

7. **Stitch the Velcro.** Trim the width of the Velcro to ⅜ inch (1 cm). Sew the hook side of
    the Velcro to the outer fabric and the loop side to the lining. If you have trouble sewing
    the Velcro, use a stitching awl or a screwdriver to assist in pushing the fabric under
    the machine.

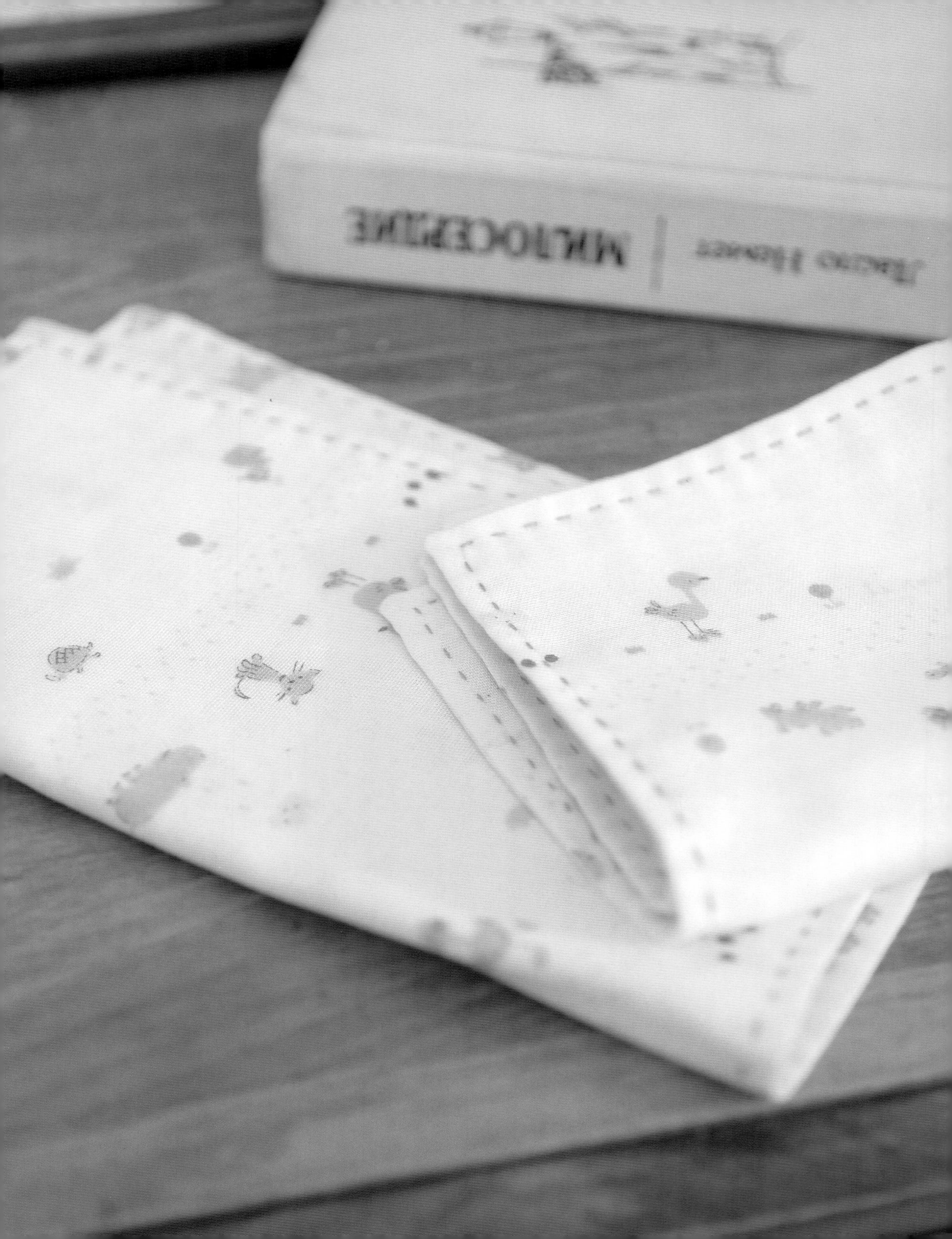

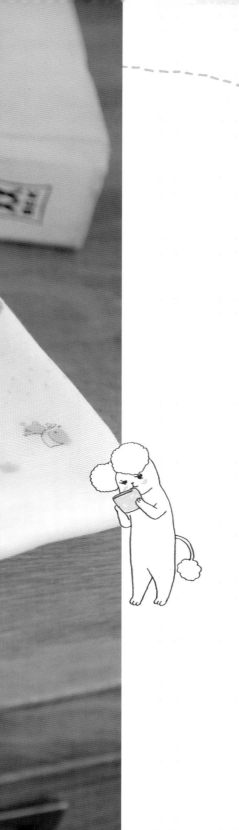

Flannel Bandanna

Your dog can have his own handkerchief that you can use for wiping the areas around his eyes and mouth to prevent staining of the fur. For a special touch, embroider your dog's name on the bandanna in a complementary color.

Flannel Bandanna

FINISHED SIZE	9⅞ x 9 inches (25 x 23 cm)
FABRIC	⅓ yard (⅓ m) double-napped flannel
NOTIONS	Embroidery floss

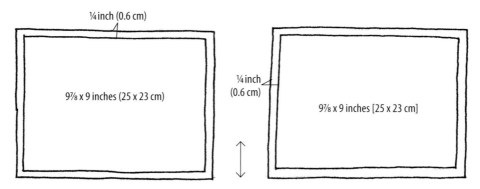

¼ inch (0.6 cm)

9⅞ x 9 inches (25 x 23 cm)

¼ inch (0.6 cm)

9⅞ x 9 inches [25 x 23 cm]

1. **Cut out the fabric pattern pieces.** Trace two 9⅞ x 9-inch (25 x 23-cm) rectangles on the wrong side of your fabric and add a ¼-inch (0.6-cm) seam allowance. Cut out the fabric pieces.

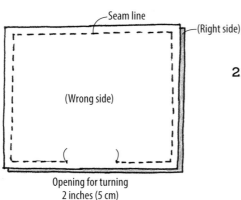

Seam line

(Right side)

(Wrong side)

Opening for turning
2 inches (5 cm)

2. **Sew the handkerchief.** Align the two fabric pieces together with right sides facing and sew them around the perimeter, leaving a 2-inch (5-cm) opening for turning.

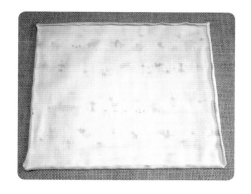

3. **Trim the seam allowance and press.** Trim the corner seam allowances, fold the seam allowances inward, and press them flat.

4. **Sharpen the corners and edges.** To achieve the sharpest corners, reach into the handkerchief and pull out one corner, turning the handkerchief right side out. Thread a needle without knotting and then stitch through the threads in the corner of the handkerchief. Use the thread to pull at the corner until it makes a perfect point, being careful not to rip your seam.

Pull the thread to make a sharp corner.

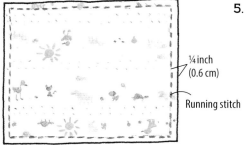

¼ inch (0.6 cm)

Running stitch

5. **Sew the topstitching.** Straighten out the rest of the seams and iron the handkerchief flat. Mark a line ¼ inch (0.6 cm) in from the outer edge of the right side of the handkerchief and sew a running stitch along the line with embroidery floss. This will also close up the opening you used for turning.

Double-napped flannel: Soft, double-napped flannel is often used to make baby products, such as blankets, bibs, and hats. It is perfect for pets with sensitive skin.

Take It with You

Tote Bag

When you take your dog on an outing, you'll need to bring some treats, some toys, clean-up bags, water, and more. Why not carry an attractive tote that's large enough to hold everything your dog needs?

Tote Bag

FINISHED SIZE	13 x 11½ inches (33 x 29 cm)
FABRIC	1¼ yards (1¼ m) linen for outer bag and lining 3 fat quarters patchwork fabric for patchwork accents
NOTIONS	1 yard (1 m) of fusible fleece interfacing ¼ yard (¼ m) of medium-weight fusible interfacing Two 14-inch (35-cm) leather handles Two decorative fabric labels One wooden button One large magnetic snap Eight metal rivets 1⅓ yards (1⅓ m) linen bias tape

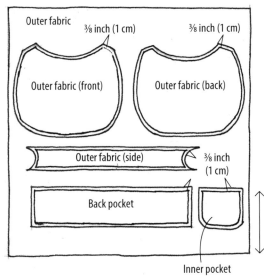

Outer fabric

⅜ inch (1 cm)　⅜ inch (1 cm)

Outer fabric (front)　Outer fabric (back)

Outer fabric (side)　⅜ inch (1 cm)

Back pocket

Inner pocket

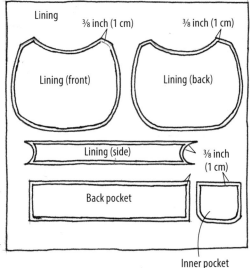

Lining

⅜ inch (1 cm)　⅜ inch (1 cm)

Lining (front)　Lining (back)

Lining (side)　⅜ inch (1 cm)

Back pocket

Inner pocket

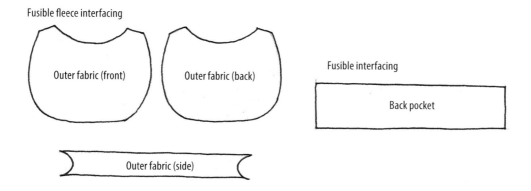

Fusible fleece interfacing

Outer fabric (front)

Outer fabric (back)

Fusible interfacing

Back pocket

Outer fabric (side)

1. **Cut out the fabric pattern pieces .** Lay the pattern pieces on the wrong side of the fabric and trace the pattern. Add a ⅜-inch (1-cm) seam allowance and then cut the fabric pieces out. For the fusible fleece interfacing and medium-weight interfacing, cut the pieces without a seam allowance.

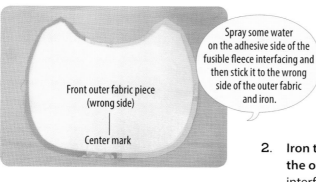

Front outer fabric piece
(wrong side)

Center mark

Spray some water on the adhesive side of the fusible fleece interfacing and then stick it to the wrong side of the outer fabric and iron.

2. **Iron the fusible fleece interfacing to the outer fabric.** Iron the fusible fleece interfacing to the wrong side of the outer fabric for the back and front bag pieces. Fold the pieces in half to find and mark the center points. You can decorate the right side of the outer bag fabric with patchwork if desired.

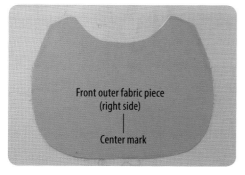

Front outer fabric piece
(right side)

Center mark

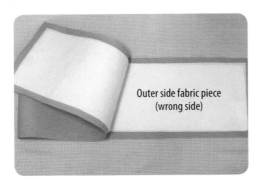
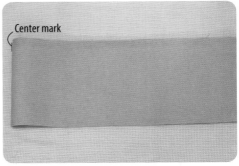

Center mark

Outer side fabric piece
(wrong side)

3.   **Back outer fabric piece (right side).** Iron the fusible interfacing to the side outer fabric piece. Iron the fusible interfacing to the outer side fabric piece as well. Fold the side piece in half to find and mark the center point.

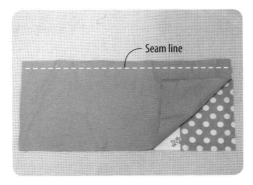

Seam line

4.   **Make the back pocket.** Create a row of patchwork with different scraps to make the back pocket. When the piece is large enough to fit the pattern, iron the fusible interfacing to the wrong side of the patchwork. Line up the patchwork with the back pocket lining and sew them together along the top edge. Press the seam allowance toward the lining and turn the pocket right side out.

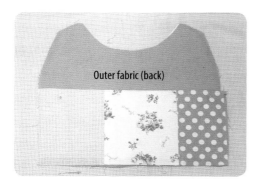

Outer fabric (back)

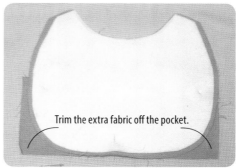

Trim the extra fabric off the pocket.

5. **Sew the back pocket on the outer fabric.** Align the pocket piece at the top of the bag's back outer fabric piece. Adjust the pocket so it is centered and lined up along the bottom and then pin it in place. Trim the excess fabric and then sew it in place along the edges and vertically along the center to create a dividing line.

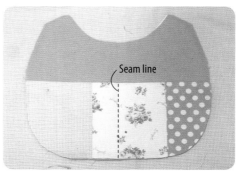

Seam line

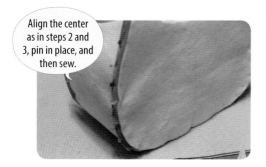

Align the center as in steps 2 and 3, pin it in place, and then sew.

6. **Join the front, back, and side pieces.** Align the side edges of the front and side pieces together with right sides facing. Sew them together along these edges and then repeat for the back piece and the other edge of the side piece. Once all of the pieces are joined, cut notches into the seam allowance at the curves and then turn the bag right side out.

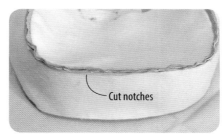

Cut notches

7. **Make the inner pocket.** You can use one piece of fabric or a patchwork of fabric scraps for the inner pocket's outer fabric and lining. Align the pocket fabric and lining together with right sides facing and sew them together around the perimeter, leaving a small opening for turning. Turn the pocket right side out and close the opening with blind stitches.

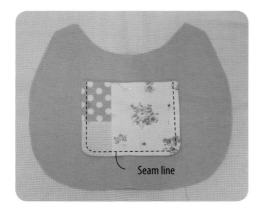

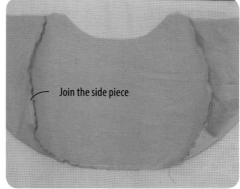

8. **Make the lining.** Decide where you'd like to place the inner pocket on your lining and then edge-stitch it in place along the sides and bottom. Join the front and back to the side piece following the instructions for the outer fabric.

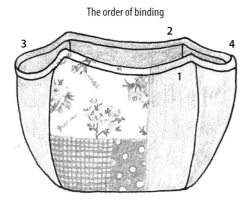

The order of binding

Bound seam finish

9. **Join the outer fabric and lining.** Put the lining fabric inside of the outer fabric with wrong sides facing. Bind the edges with bias tape, first by binding the center front and back curved edges and then by binding the left and right sides.

Front of the bag

Back of the bag

10. **Attach the fabric labels and handles.** Decorate the front of the bag with a fabric label and a wooden button. Stitch a fabric label on the back of the bag as well. Attach the magnetic snap to the inside center of the bag. To finish, attach the leather handles at the bag corners with rivets.

Ready to take a walk

Large Canvas Bag

Canvas fabric is easy to work with and strong, making a sturdy bag for outings. Make a cushioned mat that fits in the bag so that your dog can rest comfortably when you take a break. Adjust the size of this project, if needed, for the size of your dog.

Large Canvas Bag

FINISHED SIZE	16⅛ inches tall, 7 inches wide, 10¼ high (41 x 18 x 26 cm)
FABRIC	⅔ yards (⅔ m) canvas for outer bag 1¼ yards (1¼ m) striped cotton for lining ¼ yard (¼ m) faux leather for bag bottom and pocket ¼ yard (¼ m) lightweight fabric for cushioned mat
NOTIONS	⅔ yard (⅔ m) fusible fleece interfacing 12⅝ inches x 7 inches (32 x 18 cm) plastic or cardboard for bag bottom 7 inches (18 cm) of ¾-inch- (2-cm-) wide Velcro Cotton batting Straight grain binding tape Two decorative buttons One decorative fabric label

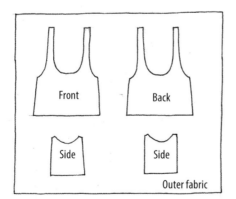

Front

Back

Side

Side

Outer fabric

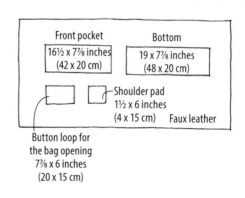

Front pocket
16½ x 7⅞ inches
(42 x 20 cm)

Bottom
19 x 7⅞ inches
(48 x 20 cm)

Shoulder pad
1½ x 6 inches
(4 x 15 cm)   Faux leather

Button loop for
the bag opening
7⅞ x 6 inches
(20 x 15 cm)

1. **Cut out the fabric pattern pieces .** Lay the front, back, and side pattern pieces on the wrong side of the fabric and trace the patterns. Trace the rest of the pattern pieces as rectangles according to the given measurements in the illustration. The seam allowances are already included in the pattern pieces and rectangles. When cutting the fusible fleece interfacing, trim off ¼ inch (0.6 cm) around all the edges. Iron the fusible fleece interfacing to the wrong side of the bag front, back, and sides.

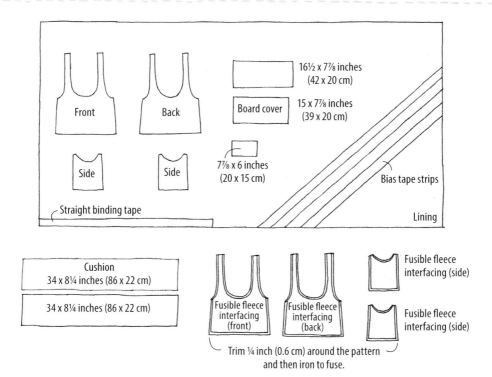

16½ x 7⅞ inches
(42 x 20 cm)

Board cover

15 x 7⅞ inches
(39 x 20 cm)

7⅞ x 6 inches
(20 x 15 cm)

Front

Back

Side

Side

Straight binding tape

Bias tape strips

Lining

Cushion
34 x 8¼ inches (86 x 22 cm)

34 x 8¼ inches (86 x 22 cm)

Fusible fleece
interfacing
(front)

Fusible fleece
interfacing
(back)

Fusible fleece
interfacing (side)

Fusible fleece
interfacing (side)

Trim ¼ inch (0.6 cm) around the pattern
and then iron to fuse.

2. **Make the front pocket.** Use the straight grain binding tape to bind the top edge of the front pocket piece.

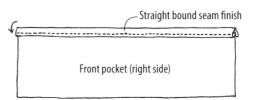

Straight bound seam finish

Front pocket (right side)

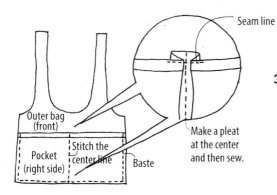

Seam line

Outer bag
(front)

Pocket
(right side)

Stitch the
center line

Baste

Make a pleat
at the center
and then sew.

3. **Attach the pocket on the outer bag.** Align the pocket from step 2 onto the outer bag front and sew it in place along the center line. Make small pleats toward the center of the bag so that the side edges align and then baste the side and bottom edges in place.

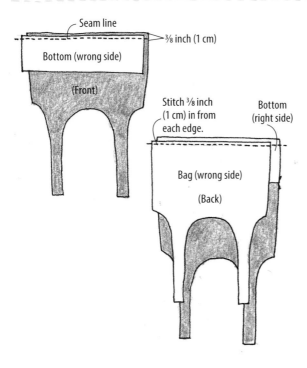

Seam line

⅜ inch (1 cm)

Bottom (wrong side)

(Front)

Stitch ⅜ inch
(1 cm) in from
each edge.

Bottom
(right side)

Bag (wrong side)

(Back)

4. **Join the front and back pieces.** Align the bottom edge of the bag front to one long edge of the bag bottom and stitch them together, starting ⅜ inch (1 cm) in from the beginning and stopping short ⅜ inch (1 cm) from the end. Edge-stitch ¹⁄₁₆ inch (0.2 cm) away from the finished seam. Repeat this with the bag back and the other long edge of the bag bottom.

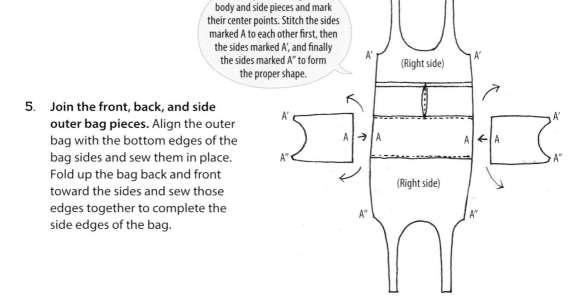

Lay out the bag body and side pieces and mark their center points. Stitch the sides marked A to each other first, then the sides marked A', and finally the sides marked A" to form the proper shape.

A'   (Right side)   A'

A'   A'

A → A   A ← A

A"   A"

(Right side)

A"   A"

5. **Join the front, back, and side outer bag pieces.** Align the outer bag with the bottom edges of the bag sides and sew them in place. Fold up the bag back and front toward the sides and sew those edges together to complete the side edges of the bag.

6. **Make the button loop at the bag opening.** Fold under the long edges of the button loop by ⅜ inch (1 cm) and then fold the whole loop in half lengthwise with wrong sides together. Sew down the folded edge and then sew the loop in place, centering it along the edge of the bag back on the right side of the opening.

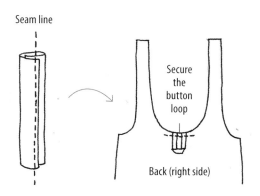

Seam line

Secure the button loop

Back (right side)

⅜ inch (1 cm)   ⅜ inch (1 cm)

Lining bottom board
(wrong side)

Seam line

Lining bottom board
(right side)

Bottom lining piece
(right side)

7. **Join the bottom board to the bottom lining piece.** Make a double-fold hem along both short edges of the board cover piece and then sew the folds in place. Center the board cover over the bottom lining piece and sew it in place along the raw edges. You can now attach the front, back, and side pieces the same as the outer bag as in steps 4 and 5.

8. **Join the outer bag and lining, part 1.** Align the outer bag and lining together with right sides facing, the outer bag inside the lining, and the wrong side of the lining facing out. Stitch them together just along the curved handle sections and then cut notches in the seam allowance. Turn the bag right side out.

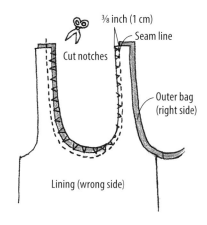

⅜ inch (1 cm)

Seam line

Cut notches

Outer bag
(right side)

Lining (wrong side)

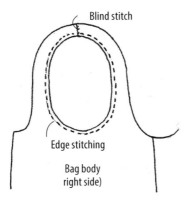

Blind stitch

Edge stitching

Bag body
right side)

9. **Join the outer bag and lining, part 2.**
Join the tips of the handle with blind
stitches, using a narrower stitch along
the lining. Edge-stitch along the seam
from step 8, $\frac{1}{16}$ inch (0.2 cm) in from
the inner edge of the handle.

10. **Join the outer bag and lining, part 3.**
Baste the outer bag and lining together
along the opening for the bag and
then bind the bag opening (including
the outer edge of the handle) with bias
tape. Sew the decorative buttons on the
pocket opening and the front side of
the bag opening. Cut the bottom board
to the proper size and insert it into the
bottom of the bag.

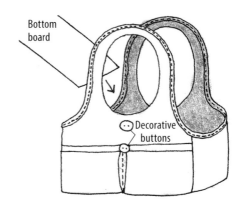

Bottom
board

Decorative
buttons

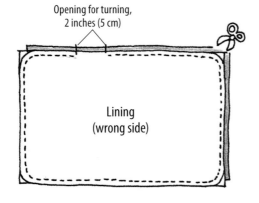

Opening for turning,
2 inches (5 cm)

Lining
(wrong side)

11. **Make the shoulder pad, part 1.** Take
the shoulder pad pieces and trim the
four corners so that they are rounded.
Layer the faux leather and the lining
together with right sides facing and
sew them together around the edges,
leaving a 2-inch (5-cm) opening for
turning. Turn the shoulder pad right
side out through the opening.

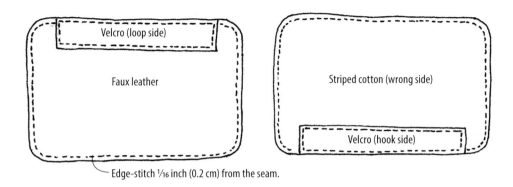

Edge-stitch ¹⁄₁₆ inch (0.2 cm) from the seam.

12. **Make the shoulder pad, part 2.** Edge-stitch along the finished seam ¹⁄₁₆ inch (0.2 cm) in from the edge of the faux leather. Sew the loop side of the Velcro onto one long side of the faux leather and sew the hook side of the Velcro onto the lining side.

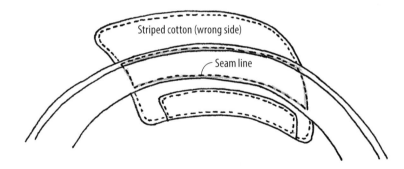

13. **Make the shoulder pad, part 3.** Mark the center of one of the shoulder straps and then center the shoulder pad on the strap. Sew it in place where the two pieces overlap.

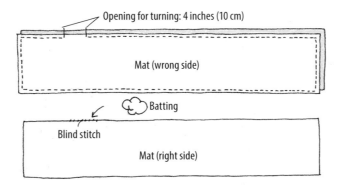

Opening for turning: 4 inches (10 cm)

Mat (wrong side)

Batting

Blind stitch

Mat (right side)

14. **Make the pad.** Layer the two pad pieces together with right sides facing and sew them together around the perimeter, leaving a 4-inch (10-cm) opening for turning. Turn the cushion right side out, fill it with batting, and then close it up with blind stitches.

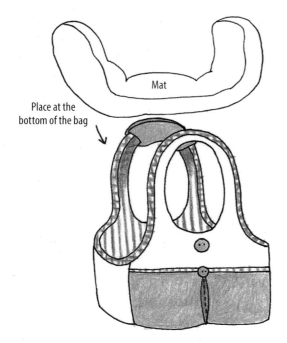

Mat

Place at the bottom of the bag

15. **Place the cushioned mat.** Place the mat in the bag to finish the project.

Picnic Blanket

It's nice to sit down and relax when you go for a walk in the park, so why not make a picnic blanket that you can take with you? It's made of waterproof fabric, so you can just brush it off when you're done, and it will be clean and ready to store in its own pouch.

 The storage pouch is also made of waterproof fabric.

How to Make

Picnic Blanket

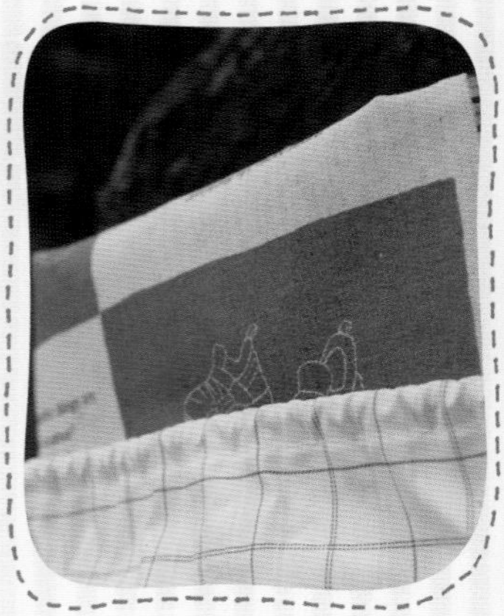

FINISHED SIZE picnic pad: 31⅛ x 42⅛ inches (79 x 107 cm)
storage bag: 9 x 13⅜ inches (23 x 34 cm)

FABRIC
- ⅔ yard (⅔ m) cotton/linen blend
- ¼ yard (¼ m) wide-striped quilting cotton (fabric A)
- ¼ yard (¼ m) striped quilting cotton (fabric B)
- ¼ yard (¼ m) narrow striped quilting cotton (fabric C)
- 1¼ yards (1¼ m) waterproof fabric

NOTIONS
- 1¼ yards (1¼ m) 1⁄16-inch- (0.2-cm-) wide cotton string
- Six decorative beads

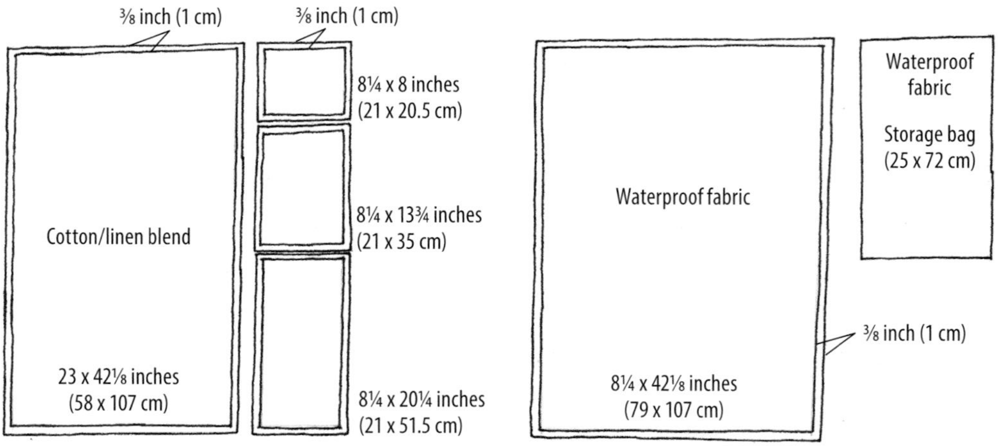

⅜ inch (1 cm)
⅜ inch (1 cm)
Cotton/linen blend
23 x 42⅛ inches
(58 x 107 cm)
8¼ x 8 inches
(21 x 20.5 cm)
8¼ x 13¾ inches
(21 x 35 cm)
8¼ x 20¼ inches
(21 x 51.5 cm)
Waterproof fabric
8¼ x 42⅛ inches
(79 x 107 cm)
⅜ inch (1 cm)
Waterproof fabric
Storage bag
(25 x 72 cm)

1. **Cut the fabric pattern pieces out.** Trace the various rectangles shown in the illustration according to the indicated measurements on the wrong side of your fabric. For the storage bag, add no seam allowance but add a ⅜-inch (1-cm) seam allowance around the edges for the rest of the pattern pieces and then cut out the fabric pieces.

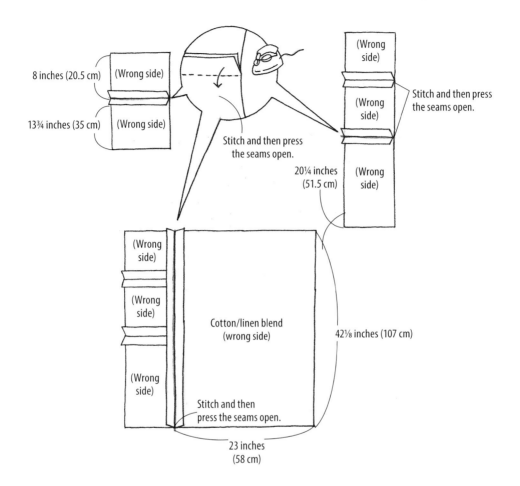

8 inches (20.5 cm)

(Wrong side)

13¾ inches (35 cm) (Wrong side)

(Wrong side)

(Wrong side)

(Wrong side)

20¼ inches (51.5 cm) (Wrong side)

Stitch and then press the seams open.

Stitch and then press the seams open.

(Wrong side)

(Wrong side)

(Wrong side)

Cotton/linen blend (wrong side)

42⅛ inches (107 cm)

Stitch and then press the seams open.

23 inches (58 cm)

2. **Sew the picnic pad.** Align the quilting fabrics A and B vertically and sew them together along the short edge. Press the seam allowance open. Next, align quilting fabric C to the bottom of fabric B and sew them together vertically, pressing the seam open. Align the patchwork piece of A, B, and C with the side of the cotton/linen fabric and sew them along the long edge. Press this seam open as well.

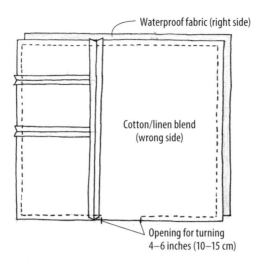

Waterproof fabric (right side)

Cotton/linen blend
(wrong side)

Opening for turning
4–6 inches (10–15 cm)

3. **Attach the waterproof fabric.** Align the picnic pad and the waterproof fabric together with right sides facing and sew them around the perimeter, leaving a 4–6-inch (10–15-cm) opening for turning.

4. **Clip the four corners and turn the right side out.** Trim the corners of the seam allowance and turn the pad right side out.

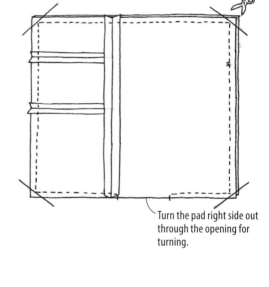

Turn the pad right side out through the opening for turning.

Edge stitching

Trim the four corners of the seam allowance.

5. **Make decorative stitches.** Straighten out the seams and iron the pad flat. Edge-stitch around the perimeter of the pad.

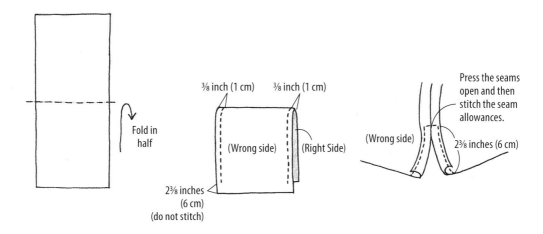

Fold in half

⅜ inch (1 cm) ⅜ inch (1 cm)

(Wrong side) (Right Side)

2⅜ inches
(6 cm)
(do not stitch)

Press the seams open and then stitch the seam allowances.

(Wrong side) 2⅜ inches (6 cm)

6. **Make the storage bag, part 1.** Fold the waterproof fabric in half widthwise with right sides together. Stitch the side edges but start 2⅜ inches (6 cm) from the top edge with a ⅜-inch (1-cm) seam allowance. Press the seams open and then stitch the top edges of the seam allowance to the bag as shown in the illustration.

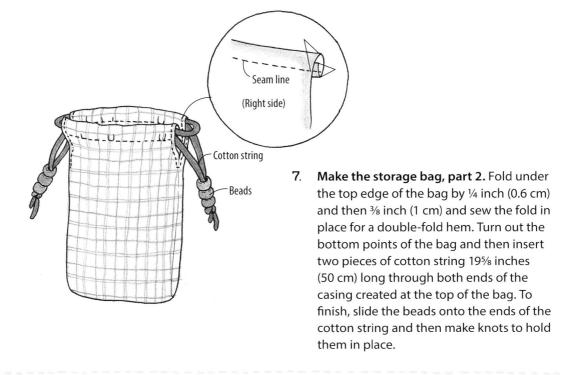

Seam line

(Right side)

Cotton string

Beads

7. **Make the storage bag, part 2.** Fold under the top edge of the bag by ¼ inch (0.6 cm) and then ⅜ inch (1 cm) and sew the fold in place for a double-fold hem. Turn out the bottom points of the bag and then insert two pieces of cotton string 19⅝ inches (50 cm) long through both ends of the casing created at the top of the bag. To finish, slide the beads onto the ends of the cotton string and then make knots to hold them in place.

sunscreen cap
for puppies

Sun Protection

Polka-Dot Visor

On a sunny day, your dog needs to shield his eyes from the UV rays just like you do. This visor is as fashionable as it is practical.

 The slide buckle and ear holes help the visor fit securely and comfortably.

Polka-Dot Visor

SIZES	XS–XL
FABRIC	¼–½ yard (¼–½ m) polka-dot cotton
NOTIONS	Slide buckle
	⅛ yard (⅛ m) medium-weight fusible interfacing

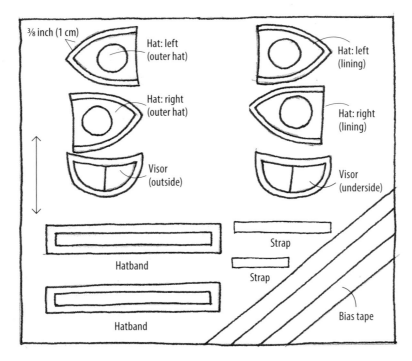

1. **Cut out the fabric pattern pieces out.** Lay the pattern pieces on the wrong side of the fabric and trace the pattern. Add a ⅜-inch (1-cm) seam allowance around the edges except for the bottom of the cap, ear holes, and hat straps. You will bind the bottom of the cap and ear holes with binding, so they need no seam allowance. Cut out the fabric pieces for the hat, along with an additional visor and hatband piece from the interfacing.

2. **Join the left and right front hat pieces.** Align the left and right outer hat pieces together with right sides facing and stitch them together along the center seam. Trim the seam allowance and cut notches at the curves.

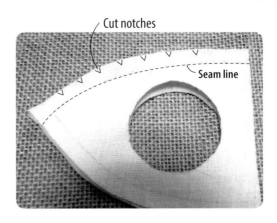

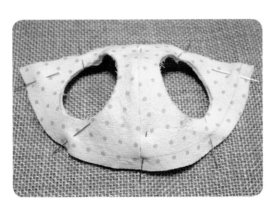

3. **Join the left and right hat lining pieces.** Use the same method in step 2 to join the lining pieces.

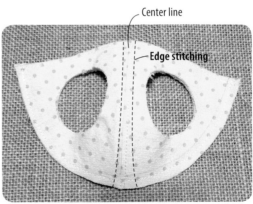

4. **Join the hat shell and lining.** Align the outer hat and lining pieces together with wrong sides facing and stitch them together with a ¼-inch (0.6-cm) seam around the perimeter. Edge-stitch ⅛ inch (0.3 cm) to the left and right of the center seam.

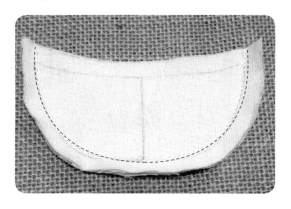 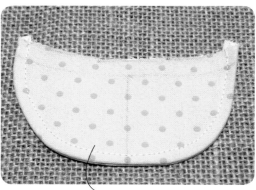

Edge stitching

5. **Make the visor.** Iron the fusible interfacing to the visor piece and then align the outer visor fabric and the lining with right sides together. Sew them together along the curved edge and then trim the seam allowance and cut notches in the curves. Turn the visor right side out and iron it flat. Complete the seam by sewing edge stitches along the completed edge.

 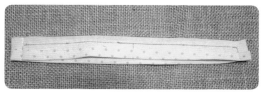

6. **Make the hatband.** Iron the interfacing to one of the hatband pieces. Align the hatband front and back pieces together with right sides facing. Fold under the seam allowance of both pieces along one long edge and iron the folds flat. Sew the two pieces together with a ⅜-inch (1-cm) seam allowance along the two short edges (creating a ring) and turn the band right side out.

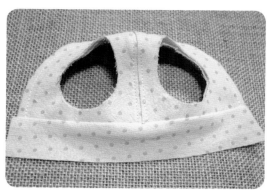

7. **Make the back hem binding, part 1.** Align the bias binding across the bottom edge of the hat with right sides together. Trim off enough bias tape so it fits the bottom edge and then sew it in place with a ¼-inch (0.6-cm) seam allowance. Press the binding away from the hat.

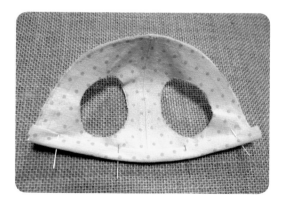
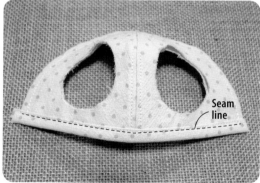

Seam
line

8. **Make the back hem binding, part 2.** Fold under the raw edge of the bias binding by ⅜ inch (1 cm) and then wrap the bias over the edge of the hat, covering the seam from the previous step. Once covered, stitch the bias binding in place again.

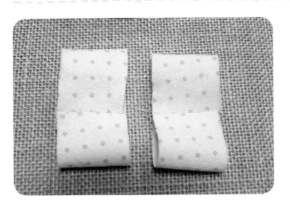

9. **Make the bias tape for the ear holes, part 1.** Measure the circumference for the ear holes and add ¾ inch (2 cm) to that measurement. Cut two bias strips at those lengths. Fold them in half widthwise and sew them together along the short edges to create rings.

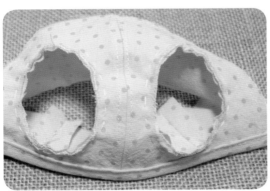

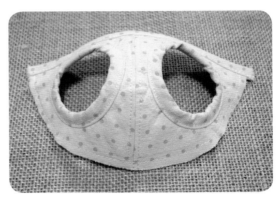

10. **Make the bias tape for the ear holes, part 2.** With right sides facing, sew the bias tape around the circumference of the ear hole with a ¼-inch (0.6-cm) seam allowance. Cut notches along the curves. Fold under the raw edge of the bias tape by ¼ inch (0.6 cm) and then fold it again, wrapping over the seam allowance to cover the previous seam. Sew the folded edge of the bias binding in place.

11. **Join the hat, visor, and hatband, part 1.** Find and mark the center point of the front hat edge and hatband. Align the raw edge of the noninterfaced side of the hatband with the hat lining and sew the edges together.

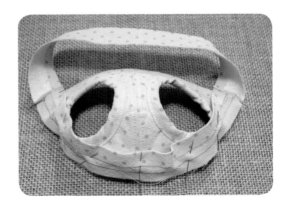

12. **Join the hat, visor, and hatband, part 2.** Trim the seam allowance of the previous seam. Turn the hat right side out and adjust the shape slightly. Center the visor over the hatband just sewn and layer the other (interfaced) side of the hatband beneath it. Match up the folded edges and pin and baste them in place.

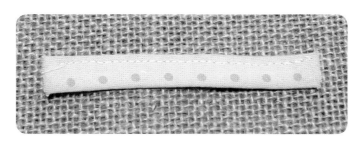

13. **Make the hat strap, part 1.** Fold under ⅜ inch (1 cm) along each long edge of the short strap and press the folds. Fold the strap again in half lengthwise with wrong sides together and press. Edge-stitch the folds in place and then loop the slide buckle through it.

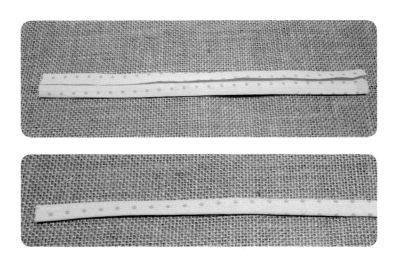

14. **Make the hat strap, part 2.** Take the long hat strap and also fold under each long edge by ⅜ inch (1 cm). Next, fold the whole strap in half lengthwise with wrong sides together and press. After pressing, edge-stitch the folds in place.

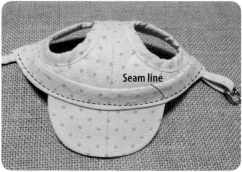

Seam line

15. **Sew the hat straps on the hat.** Layer the short strap beneath the right corner of the hat and the long strap beneath the left. Sew the straps in place from the right side.

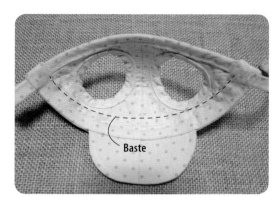

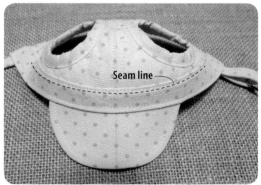

16. **Make decorative stitches.** Turn the hat to the wrong side, fold in the extra seam allowance at the top of the visor, and baste it in place. Turn the hat right side up and edge-stitch the top edge, anchoring the basted fold.

Lovely neck collar

Fancy Collar

It is easy to make a decorative neck collar that your dog can wear along with his regular collar. Attach it with a simple hook closure and, voilà, your pup looks stylish for his walks around the block or wherever you go together.

Fancy Collar

SIZES	XS–XL
FABRIC	Round Collar: ⅛–¼ yard (⅛–¼ m) striped cotton/linen blend
	Pointed Collar: ⅛–¼ yard (⅛–¼ m) striped cotton blend
	⅛–¼ yard (⅛–¼ m) denim for lining
NOTIONS	Round collar: 13–22 inches (33–56 cm) narrow decorative lace
	Both: ⅛–¼ yard (⅛–¼ m) lightweight fusible interfacing
	Both: Hook and eye closure

Make the round collar.

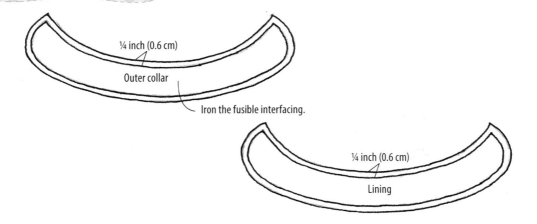

¼ inch (0.6 cm)

Outer collar

Iron the fusible interfacing.

¼ inch (0.6 cm)

Lining

1. **Lining.** Cut out the fabric pattern pieces. Lay the pattern pieces on the wrong side of the fabric and trace the pattern. Add a ¼-inch (0.6-cm) seam allowance. Cut the collar pieces from the fabric as well as one collar piece from the interfacing. Iron the fusible interfacing to the wrong side of the outer collar fabric.

2. **Secure the lace in place.** Align the outer collar and lining together with right sides facing. Tuck the lace between the outer fabric and the lining, then wrap the lace around the edges pointing towards the inside of the collar. Pin the lace strip in place.

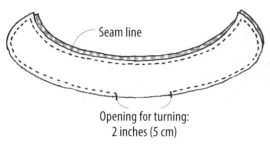

Seam line

Opening for turning:
2 inches (5 cm)

3. **Sew the lace strip in place.** Sew the collar pieces together around the perimeter, leaving a 2-inch (5-cm) opening for turning. Stitch the curved edges with a smaller stitch length to ensure the best shape. Cut notches along the curved seam allowances except for the opening.

4. **Edge-stitch the seam.** Turn the collar right side out through the opening. Flatten out the seams, adjust the collar shape, and sew edge stitches ⅛ inch (0.3 cm) around the finished seam.

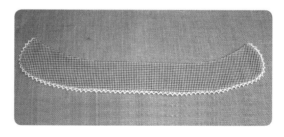

5. **Install the hook and eye.** Stitch the hook and the eye on the back of the collar.

Make the pointed collar.

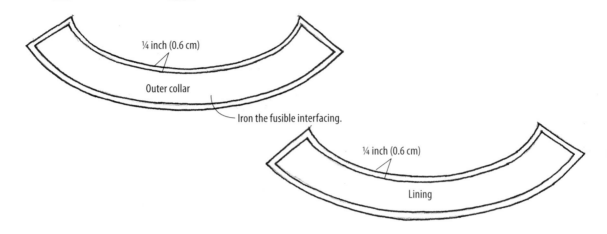

¼ inch (0.6 cm)

Outer collar

Iron the fusible interfacing.

¼ inch (0.6 cm)

Lining

1. **Cut the fabric pattern pieces out.** Lay the pattern pieces on the wrong side of the fabric and trace the pattern. Add a ¼-inch (0.6-cm) seam allowance around all of the edges. Cut out the collar pieces from the fabric and one collar piece from the interfacing. Iron the fusible interfacing to the wrong side of the lining.

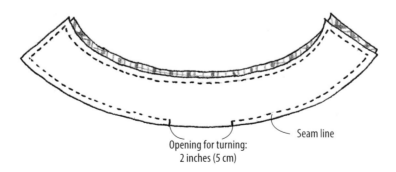

Opening for turning:
2 inches (5 cm)

Seam line

2. **Join the outer collar and lining.** Align the outer collar and lining together with right sides facing and sew around the perimeter, leaving a 2-inch (5-cm) opening for turning.

3. **Cut notches.** Cut notches along the curved seam allowance except for the opening. Clip the four corners.

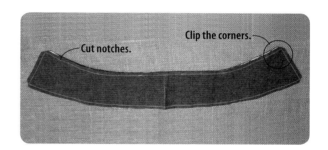

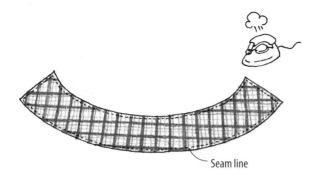

Seam line

4. **Adjust the seam and edge-stitch.** Turn the collar right side out through the opening. Poke out the four corners completely and then iron them flat. Edge-stitch around the finished seam ⅛ inch (0.3 cm) from the edge.

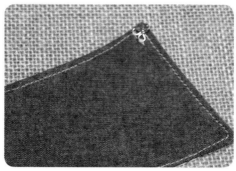

5. **Attach the hook and eye.** Stitch the hook and the eye on the back of the collar.

Triangular Scarf

This simple triangular scarf is easy to make and easy to wear, made from comfortable, soft flannel. It can also be used as a handkerchief for puppies.

♥ Use the scarf as an extra piece of identification by including your pup's name and contact info.

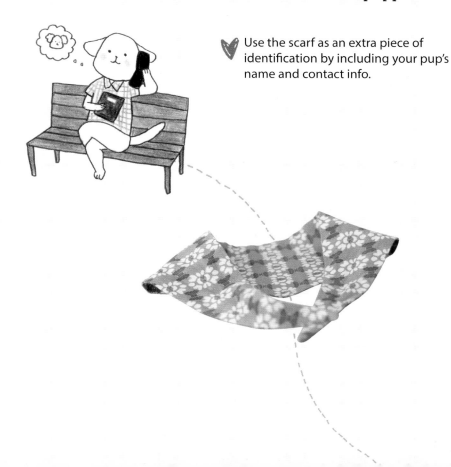

Triangular Scarf

SIZES XS–XL

FABRIC ⅛–¼ yards (⅛–¼ m) lightweight flannel

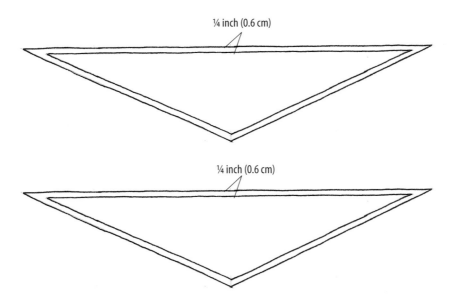

¼ inch (0.6 cm)

¼ inch (0.6 cm)

1. **Cut out the fabric pattern pieces .** Lay the pattern pieces on the wrong side of the fabric and trace the patterns, adding a ¼-inch (0.6-cm) seam allowance along all edges. Cut out the fabric pieces.

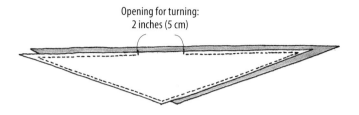

Opening for turning:
2 inches (5 cm)

2. **Sew the scarf.** Align the two triangular scarf pieces together with right sides facing and sew them together around the perimeter, leaving a 2-inch (5-cm) opening for turning.

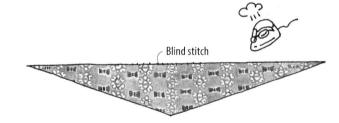

Blind stitch

3. **Turn the scarf right side out and iron.** Turn the scarf right side out through the opening and iron it flat. To finish, close up the opening with blind stitches. Because light flannel can tear easily, be very careful while sewing.

You can stitch a fabric label with your dog's name onto the scarf or embroider your name and contact number on it.

Ruffled Cape

If you're looking for an item that is fashionable but not too dressy, a cape is perfect. I use seasonal prints to make a variety of capes for year-round style.

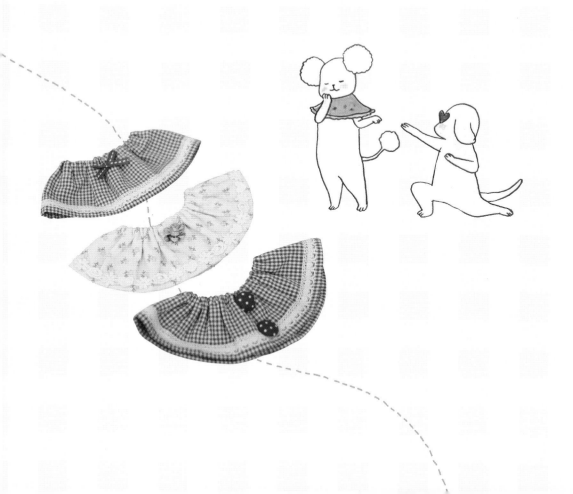

Ruffled Cape

SIZES	XS–XL
FABRIC	⅛–¼ yard (⅛–¼ m) striped cotton/linen blend
NOTIONS	¾–1 yard (¾–1 m) narrow decorative lace About 1 yard (1 m) narrow elastic Two fabric-covered buttons

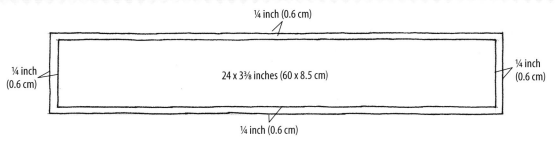

¼ inch (0.6 cm)

¼ inch (0.6 cm)

¼ inch (0.6 cm)

24 x 3⅜ inches (60 x 8.5 cm)

1. **Cut out the fabric pattern pieces .** Lay the pattern pieces on the wrong side of the fabric and trace around them. Add a ¼ inch (0.6 cm) seam allowance around all of the edges. Cut out the fabric pieces. If you prefer a cape with more ruffles, increase the width of the pattern.

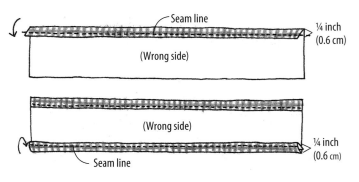

Seam line

¼ inch (0.6 cm)

(Wrong side)

(Wrong side)

¼ inch (0.6 cm)

Seam line

2. **Fold under top and bottom and then sew.** Fold under the top edge of the cape by ¼ inch (0.6 cm) and then the bottom edge by ⅝ inch (1.5 cm) twice. Press the folds in place and then sew them in place.

3. **Sew the lace.** Sew the decorative lace ⅜ inch (1 cm) above the folded bottom edge.

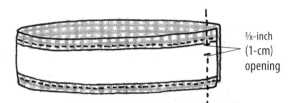

⅜-inch (1-cm) opening

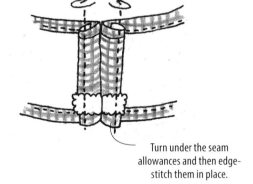

Turn under the seam allowances and then edge-stitch them in place.

4. **Stitch the side line.** Align the short side edges of the cape together with right sides facing and then sew them together, leaving a ⅜-inch (1-cm) opening for inserting the elastic. Press the seam allowances open and then fold them inward and edge-stitch them in place.

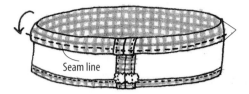

Seam line

5. **Leave an eyehole.** Fold under the top edge of the cape (the edge with the ¼-inch (0.6-cm) fold) by ¾ inch (2 cm) and then sew the fold in place right along the previous seam from step 2.

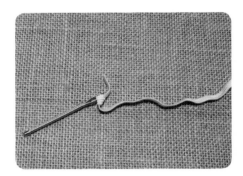

6. **Insert the elastic.** Cut the elastic a bit longer than the circumference of your dog's neck so that the cape will have a comfortable fit. Insert the elastic strip into the opening with the bodkin needle. Thread the elastic through, overlap the ends by ⅝ inch (1.5 cm), and sew them together. Close up the opening with blind stitches.

7. **Attach the buttons.** Stitch the fabric-covered buttons to the center of the cape for decoration.

Bow Tie

A classic bow tie is always in style, and the following patterns show you how to make two different types. For this project, you can bring new life to old neckties by recycling the fabric.

Note: Follow the same steps for the triangular and butterfly bow ties. Both types are made the same way; the only difference is their shape.

Bow Tie

SIZES	XS–XL
FABRIC	⅛ yard (⅛m) silk
NOTIONS	⅛ yard (⅛m) lightweight fusible interfacing
	Slide buckle
	D-ring

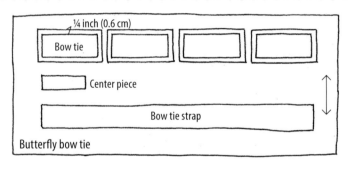

¼ inch (0.6 cm)

Bow tie

Center piece

Bow tie strap

Butterfly bow tie

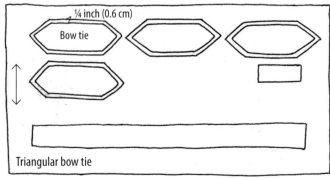

¼ inch (0.6 cm)

Bow tie

Triangular bow tie

1. **Cut the fabric pattern pieces out.** Lay the pattern pieces on the wrong side of the fabric and trace the pattern. Add ¼-inch (0.6-cm) seam allowances to the bow tie pieces but not to the center section or the strap. Cut the fabric pieces out as well as two additional bow pieces from the interfacing.

2. **Iron the fusible interfacing.** Iron the fusible interfacing to two out of four of the bow tie pieces.

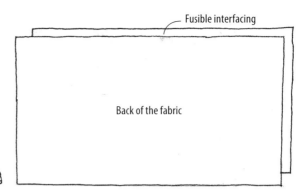

Fusible interfacing

Back of the fabric

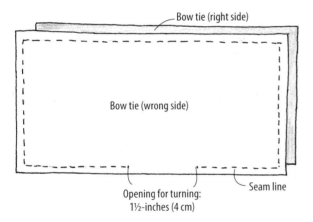

Bow tie (right side)

Bow tie (wrong side)

Opening for turning:
1½-inches (4 cm)

Seam line

3. **Sew.** Align one of the non-interfaced bow tie pieces with an interfaced piece with right sides together. Sew them together around the perimeter, leaving a 1½-inch (4-cm) opening for turning.

4. **Turn the bow tie right side out and turn out the corners.** Trim the excess seam allowance and clip the four corners. Press the seams and then turn the bow tie right side out through the opening.

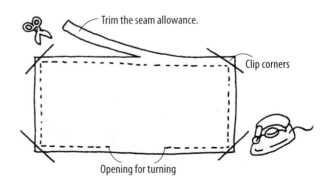

Trim the seam allowance.

Clip corners

Opening for turning

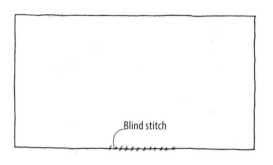

Blind stitch

5. **Adjust the shape and close the opening for turning.** Carefully pull out the edges and corners completely; you can use a needle and thread for this if needed. Iron the right side of the bow tie and then close the opening with blind stitches. Repeat to make a second bow tie.

6. **Make the center piece and adjust the shape of the bow tie.** Fold under ¼ inch (0.6 cm) on both ends of the center piece and press it flat. Find the center of the bow ties and then, with the interfaced side facing out, cinch the ties together and stitch the ties tightly in place with matching thread.

7. **Wrap the bow tie with the center piece.** Wrap the center piece around the center of the bow tie and secure it in place by hand-stitching on the back with a blind stitch. The adjustable strap will loop through this center piece, so make sure it's not wrapped around the bow tie too tightly or loosely.

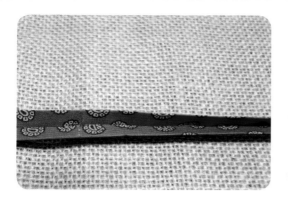 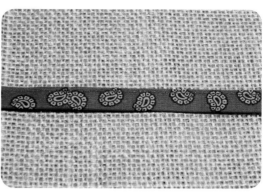

8. **Make the strap.** Mark two lines going in ¼ inch (0.6 cm) from each long edge of the strap. Fold the fabric inward along this fold line and then fold the entire strap in half lengthwise with wrong sides together. Press the folds and then edge-stitch them together. Because the fabric is very thin, it helps to pull it slightly while sewing.

9. **Install the D-ring.** Slide the strap through the center piece made in step 7. Put one end of the strap through the D-ring, fold over ⅜–⅝ inch (1–1.5 cm), and sew it in place with overcast stitches.

What Is Silk?

Silk is a kind of fabric usually used to make scarves or neck ties. It is soft and thin with an indistinct gloss on its surface. The more you wash it, the softer it becomes.

10. **Finishing.** Loop the other end of the strap through the slide buckle and then through the D-ring. Slide the strap through the middle bar of the slide buckle. To finish, fold under the end of the strap and sew it in place with overcast stitches.

11. **Adjust the length.** After you've completed all of the steps, check to make sure that you can adjust the length of the collar.

Small Carrier with Pocket

If you want to carry your small dog, you'll find this carrier easy to wear for long periods. Shoulder pads make the bag comfortable for you, while a cushioned lining makes it comfortable for your dog.

Small Carrier with Pocket

FINISHED SIZE	12¼ inches (31 cm) tall, 10⅝ inches (27 cm) high (including straps, 13¾ inches [35cm] high) and 7 inches (18 cm) wide
FABRIC	1¼ yards (1¼ m) herringbone tweed for outer bag ¼ yard (¼ m) linen for pocket
NOTIONS	⅔ yard (⅔ m) fusible fleece interfacing 1⅓ yards (1⅓ m) 1⅛-inch- (3-cm-) wide webbing 12–16 inches (30–40 cm) of ⅜-inch- (1 cm-) wide belt for safety leash 10 inches (2 5cm) of ⅝-inch- (1.5-cm-) wide leather strap 1⅔ yards (1⅔ m) cotton drawstring 1½ yards (1½ m) piping Cotton batting Two slide buckles for shoulder straps Two large D-rings One small D-ring Two large swivel hooks Two small swivel hooks Two wooden beads Two small round eyelets Three rivets Two snap buttons 12¼ x 7-inch (31 x 18-cm) plastic or cardboard for bottom of bag

1. **Cut out the fabric pattern pieces.** Lay the pattern pieces on the wrong side of the fabric and trace the patterns. For the pocket pieces, add a ⅜-inch (1-cm) seam allowance along the top and bottom edges. Add a ⅜-inch (1-cm) seam allowance around all sides for the rest of the fabric and then cut the pieces out. Cut the fusible fleece in the same way but with no seam allowances. Iron the fusible fleece interfacing to the wrong side of the outer bag fabric (front, back, side, and bottom) and the wrong side of the shoulder pad fabric.

> **Note:** This bag is suitable for dogs that weigh less than 6½ pounds (3 kg). If your dog is much smaller, you can reduce the height of the bag or make the cushion thicker.

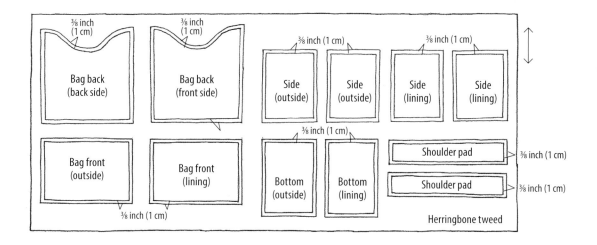

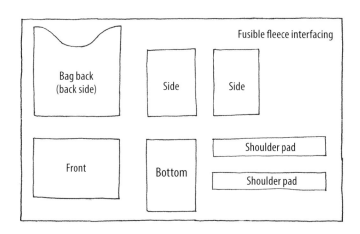

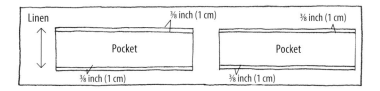

2. **Make the pocket.** Align the outer pocket and pocket lining pieces together with right sides facing and stitch them together along the upper edge (what will be the pocket opening). Turn the pocket right side out and edge-stitch along the previous seam.

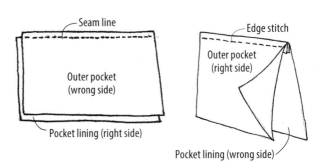

Seam line

Outer pocket (wrong side)

Pocket lining (right side)

Edge stitch

Outer pocket (right side)

Pocket lining (wrong side)

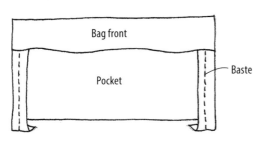

Bag front

Pocket

Baste

3. **Sew the pocket on the bag front.** Align the pocket on the outer bag front piece and center it along the bottom edge. Fold under the left and right edges of the pocket so that the seam lines of the bag front and pocket line up. Stitch the pocket to the bag front along the side and bottom edges.

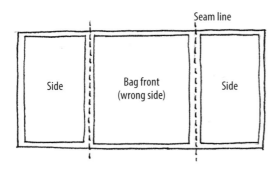

Seam line

Side

Bag front (wrong side)

Side

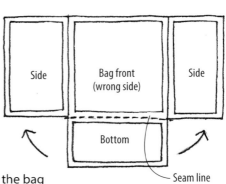

Side

Bag front (wrong side)

Side

Bottom

Seam line

4. **Join the front, side, and bottom pieces.** Align the bag sides to each side of the bag front (with attached pocket) and then sew the three pieces together in a row. Align the bag bottom beneath the bag front as the illustration shows and then sew the pieces together. Fold the sides and bottom upward so that their short edges meet and sew them together.

5. **Join the outer bag and lining, part 1.** Repeat the previous step with the lining pieces to attach the sides and bottom. When finished, put the lining into the outer bag with right sides facing. Tuck the safety leash between the layers with the end of the leash pointing down. Sew the two layers together along the upper edge.

Pocket lining (right side)

Put in

Seam line

Safety leash

Outer bag (right side)

Outer pocket (wrong side)

Round eyelet

Seam line

Outer bag (right side)

Drawstring

Seam line

5 cm

Drawstring

Outer bag (right side)

6. **Join the outer bag and lining, part 2.** Turn the bag front right side out and edge-stitch the finished seam. Install the two eyelets spaced ¾ inch (2 cm) apart at the center of the bag front, going through the outer bag layer only, not the lining. Cut the drawstrings to two 27–29-inch (70–75-cm) pieces and thread them through the eyelets with a safety pin. Allow about ¾ inch (2 cm) to extend beyond the bag front's raw edges. While keeping the drawstring nestled against the top edge as seen in the illustration, sew the outer bag front and lining together 2 inches (5 cm) below the top edge, encasing the drawstring.

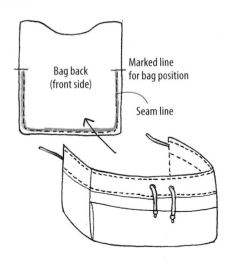

Bag back (front side)

Marked line for bag position

Seam line

7. **Join the bag front and back pieces.** Align the side and bottom edges of the bag front and back pieces. Sew the three sides together with the lining and the front side of the bag back facing each other.

8. **Install the D-rings and the piping.** Loop the 4-inch (10-cm) straps through the two large D-rings and sew each one firmly on both sides of the bag, near the bottom corners. Sew the piping along the edge of the bag back (front side). You may want to use a piping foot here. Cut notches at the curved seam allowances.

Piping

Bag back (front side)

5 cm

D-ring

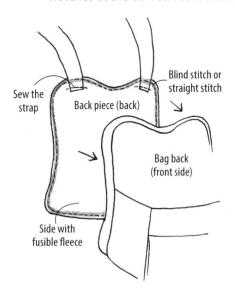

Sew the strap

Back piece (back)

Blind stitch or straight stitch

Bag back (front side)

Side with fusible fleece

9. **Join the shoulder straps and bag back (back side).** Determine where you'd like to apply the shoulder straps on the bag back (the back side, with the fusible fleece applied). Sew the straps in place on the wrong side of the fabric, and then cut notches at the seam allowance curves. Align the raw edges of both bag back pieces (front and back), fold under the seam allowances around the edges, and blind-stitch the edges together.

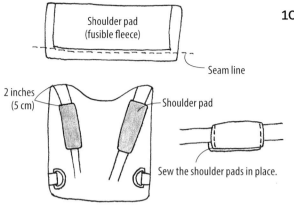

Shoulder pad
(fusible fleece)

Seam line

2 inches
(5 cm)

Shoulder pad

Sew the shoulder pads in place.

10. **Sew the shoulder pads in place and attach the bag buckles, part 1.** Fold the shoulder pads in half lengthwise and sew them together along the long edge. Turn both shoulder pads right side out and thread them through the straps. Pin them in place when they are 2 inches (5 cm) from the top of the straps. Fold in the seam allowance at the bottom and top edges and then sew them together along the folded edges, anchoring them to the straps in the process.

11. **Sew the shoulder pads in place and attach the bag buckles, part 2.** Assemble the adjustable strap by sliding the strap through the slide buckle, and then through the swivel hook, and then around the middle bar of the slide buckle again. Fold the strap over and sew it in place to finish.

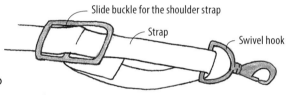

Slide buckle for the shoulder strap

Strap

Swivel hook

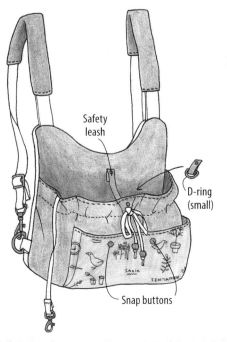

Safety leash

D-ring
(small)

Snap buttons

12. **Finishing.** Install the small swivel hook on one end of the safety-leash belt. Attach it to the bag with a rivet about 2 inches (5 cm) below the top edge of the bag back. Take a bit of the leftover leash leather and loop it through the small D-ring. Secure it inside the bag front, to the left of the eyelets, with another rivet. Install snaps or buttons on the front pockets. Slide wooden beads through the drawstrings and hold them in place with knots. To finish, add a bottom board and cushion; refer to page 117 for instructions on this.

Floral Bonnet

This lovely bonnet in a cheerful floral pattern is perfect for an outing on a spring day. Your pooch is certain to turn heads as you enjoy the fresh air together.

Floral Bonnet

FINISHED SIZE	Medium
FABRIC	24 x 24 inches (60 x 60 cm) patchwork linen fabric
NOTIONS	Fabric adhesive

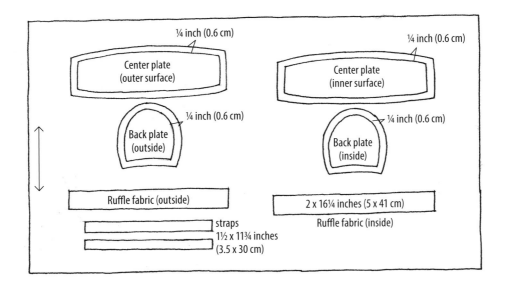

1. **Foundation.** Draw a pattern on the inner side of the prepared fabric. The sizes of the brim and straps include the seam allowance.

2. **Attach the fabric adhesive.** Iron the outer center plate and the outer back plate.

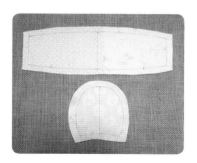

3. **Start the ruffle on the center plate.** Baste across the bottom of the center plate so that the stitches start 1½ inches (4 cm) to the left of the center line and end 1½ inches (4 cm) to the right of the center line. Pull on the thread to gather.

4. **Attaching the center plate to the outer back.** Place the center plate and outer back of the ruffled bonnet together with right sides facing. Pin at the center and both corners. Align the curved portion evenly, pin, and stitch the pieces together with a ¼-inch (0.6-cm) seam allowance.

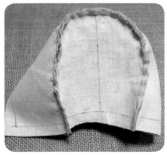

5. **Attaching the center plate to the back plate (inner).** Connect the lining the same way you did the outer pieces. I used a ¼-inch (0.6-cm) seam allowance and stitched at ⅜-inch (1-cm) intervals. At this stage, clip the extra seam allowance on the inner and outer bonnet pieces.

6. **Create the ruffled visor, part 1.** Place the inner and outer ruffle fabric together with wrong sides facing. Stitch three sides together: the two short ends and one of the long sides. (The other long side will be attached to the center plate of the bonnet.)

7. **Create the ruffled visor, part 2.** Turn the visor right-side out, press, and then topstitch over the three seams. Gather the fabric to make ruffles by basting the unstitched sides together and gently pulling the thread. Leave 4–6 inches (10–15 cm) of space on each end.

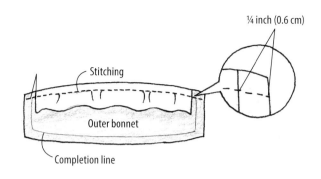

Stitching

¼ inch (0.6 cm)

Outer bonnet

Completion line

8. **Attaching the ruffle to the outer bonnet.** Adjust the ruffles so that they are distributed evenly by matching the center and both ends of the outer edges of the bonnet and the visor. Baste the two pieces together. The visor will be about ¼ inch (0.6 cm) from the left and right edge of the bonnet.

9. **Create the bonnet's straps.** Fold one short end of one strap fabric piece in ⅜ inch (1 cm) and press. Then fold both long sides of the strap fabric piece in ¼ inch (0.6 cm) and press. Next, fold the entire strap in half lengthwise, press, and topstitch the open sides. Because the strap is very narrow, you will need to slowly guide the needle of the sewing machine close to the end of the fabric. Follow the same procedure for the second strap.

10. **Attaching the outer bonnet and lining, part 1.** The bonnet's outer surface and the lining's right side will face each other. The ruffles attached to the outer surface will be sandwiched between the two pieces. Make sure the pieces match up and the ruffles are easily tucked away, but do not pin yet.

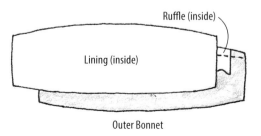

Ruffle (inside)

Lining (inside)

Outer Bonnet

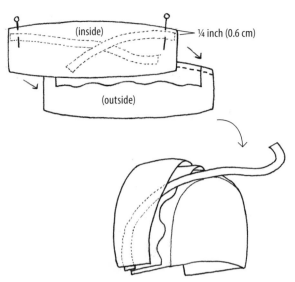

(inside)

¼ inch (0.6 cm)

(outside)

11. **Attaching the outer bonnet and lining, part 2.** Put one bonnet strap on each side, between the lining and the outer material; make sure to match raw sides together. Pin the straps in place ¼ inch (0.6 cm) from each edge.

12. **Finishing.** Stitch raw edges together, leaving about 2 inches (5 cm) open at the back plate; turn right-side out through the hole. Press, tucking in the raw seams in at the hole. Topstitch around the hat, keeping close to the edge.

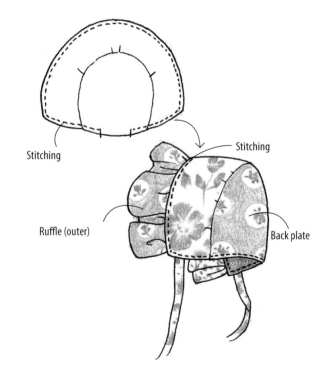

Stitching

Stitching

Ruffle (outer)

Back plate

special hat for my puppy

Fleece Hat

This soft fleece hat will protect your pup's head and ears when it's cold outside, and it looks cute, too!

How to Make

Fleece Hat

FINISHED SIZE	XS–XL
FABRIC	¼ yard (¼ m) white fleece fabric ¼ yard (¼ m) pink fleece fabric
NOTIONS	½ yard (½ m) brown leather cord ½ yard (½ m) white leather cord Cotton batting Two decorative bear-shaped buttons Two decorative pom-poms Two decorative pearl buttons Two decorative crocheted flowers Invisible thread

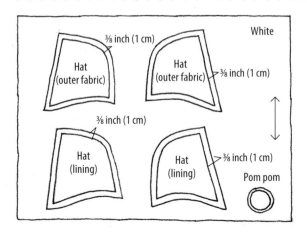

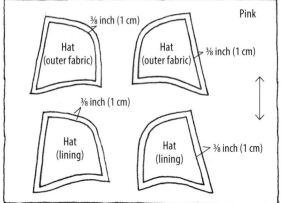

1. **Cut out the fabric pattern pieces.** Lay the pattern pieces on the wrong side of the white fleece fabric and trace the pattern. Add a ⅜-inch (1-cm) seam allowance and then cut out the fabric pieces.

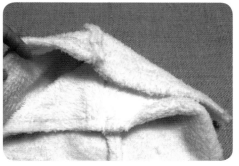

2. **Join the outer hat and lining pieces.** Align the two outer hat pieces together with right sides facing and sew them along the curved edge. Do the same with the two lining pieces. After sewing, trim and notch the seam allowance; press the outer hat seam allowance to one side and the lining to the other. Line up the center seam allowances of the outer hat and lining with right sides together and pin in place.

3. **Join the outer hat and lining.** Sew the outer hat and lining together along the edges, leaving a 2–2⅜-inch (5–6-cm) opening for turning on the bottom edge.

4. **Turn the hat right side out and edge-stitch.** Trim and notch the seam allowances and then turn the hat right side out through the opening. Fold in the seam allowance in the opening and edge-stitch around the perimeter of the hat, closing up the opening.

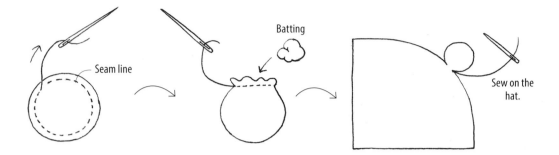

Seam line

Batting

Sew on the hat.

5. **Make the pom-pom for the hat.** Take the pom-pom fabric piece and sew a running stitch around the edges. Cinch up the pom-pom while filling it with batting. Cinch the pom-pom closed and then sew it to the hat.

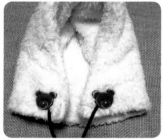

6. **Attach buttons and pom-poms.** Sew a decorative bear-shaped button and a length of brown leather cord to each of the two corners of the hat. Tie the decorative pom-poms to the ends of the leather cords.

7. **Make the pink fleece hat.** Follow the same steps to make another fleece hat in pink with white leather cords. Use the pearl buttons in place of the bear-shaped buttons and sew the decorative flowers to the ends of the leather cords.

Meet the Dogs

Ari

Breed: Shih Tzu
Age: 5
Gender: F
Characteristics: She is a short-haired girl with a pair of bright and intelligent eyes, a compact figure, and silky-soft hair. Her personality, however, is like a tomboy. But sometimes she can also be affectionate, tender, and soft. It totally depends on her mood.

See more Ari!

blog.naver.com/naanhye8098

Breed: Shih Tzu
Age: 8
Gender: F
Characteristics: With an innocent and romantic personality, Chiu-Chiu likes to make friends with people and dogs. When it comes time for a stroll, she happily jumps around like a rabbit. She is so timid that she is afraid of plastic bags. When taking a stroll, however, she fears nothing and no one!

Chiu-Chiu

A-Dong

Breed: English Cocker Spaniel
Age: 9
Gender: F
Characteristics: She has a sincere appearance and a gentle personality. She is very intelligent, like a model student: even without special training, she knows what to do. She is very into soccer balls.

See more A-Dong!

blog.naver.com/mn1853

Natto

Breed: Maltese
Age: 2
Gender: M
Characteristics: He is a little devil in angel's clothing. Even though he has an innocent appearance, he is actually a troublemaker! But he always treats his little sister as a friend. He is good at biting off dolls' noses.

See more Natto!

fullmoon1977.blog.me

Dor Kong

Breed: Shih Tzu
Age: 3
Gender: M
Characteristics: When Dor Kong was still a baby, because his front teeth didn't come in for a long time, his mom often massaged his gums with her fingers. One time he gently bit his mom's fingers. This is probably his way of showing his affection. He hates to leave his mom and is always clinging to her like chewing gum.

See more Dor Kong

blog.naver.com/der_nachhall

Breed: Toy Poodle
Age: 3
Gender: F
Characteristics: Her interest is running! If a national running race for dogs is ever held, Fei-Fei will win first place. Her appearance often gives a mistaken impression of being taciturn, but she is actually very lively and outgoing.

See more Fei-Fei!

yourlucia.blog.me

Fei-Fei

Breed: Maltese
Age: 5
Gender: F
Characteristics: With a pair of dark liquid-brown eyes, beautiful long lashes, and a long, smooth tail, she looks innocent and lovely. Although she looks a bit aloof, as soon as Aroya glances back, anyone will have a crush on her.

Aroya

Furryhead

Breed: Yorkie
Age: 9
Gender: M
Characteristics: He shows his preferences clearly and was born with rude manners. He is well known as "Malingering Devil King" at the veterinarian's office. His way of getting attention is to stick his tongue out and express innocence in his eyes.

See more Furryhead!

blog.naver.com/tingk70

Little Moon

Breed: Maltese
Age: 3
Gender: F
Characteristics: With spotless soft white hair, a slender body, and bright and intelligent eyes, Little Moon is a beauty among dogs. She doesn't look very easygoing, but she is actually naughty and playful. She may look easygoing, but she is actually naughty and playful! She loves eating, and also teasing her younger brother, Little Star.

See more Little Moon!

blog.naver.com/83187love

Pully

Breed: Toy Poodle
Age: 7
Gender: F
Characteristics: She is a master of being affectionate—and sometimes of making trouble. But Pully actually is very clever and considerate, as long as she gets a good daily walk. Her mom and older sister can tell she is very happy just through her eyes.

See more Pully!

blog.naver.com/jjrs

Little Nine

Breed: Yorkie
Age: 9
Gender: M
Characteristics: He thinks he is human and is very polite: before going into a room, he will knock on the door first. His likes to peek in on his mom while she puts on makeup. His favorite things are chicken brisket jerky and his older sister Totto.

See more Little Nine!

fullmoon1977.blog.me

Milu

Breed: Miniature Pinscher
Age: 5
Gender: M
Characteristics: He often stares at his dad, whining to get snacks. When he finishes the food in his bowl, Milu will look very sad. He is a master of looking pitiful to get what he wants.

See more Milu!

blog.naver.com/hjh9313

Index

Photo Credits

Front cover: cynoclub/Shutterstock
Front and back covers top border: Photoroyalty/Shutterstock
Background pages 1, 4: Photoroyalty/Shutterstock
Background pages 2, 3, 6, 7, 8, 9, 16, 17, 36, 37,184-189: franssonkane/Shutterstock
Page 6: monticello/Shutterstock
Page 10: Igor_S/Shutterstock
Page 12: valzan 12/Shutterstock
Page 15: Szasz-Fabian Ilka Erik/Shutterstock
Page 22: kariphoto/Shutterstock
Pages 86, 87: nemlazapaws/Shutterstock

About the Author

The author's dogs, Furryhead and Gucci.

Jisu Lee (known as Tingk)

Years ago, Tingk worked at an editorial design company, but she left her job after she got married. During the first year of her marriage, she adopted her first pets, Jjanga (Furryhead) and Gujji (Gucci), and she started learning handicrafts.

When Tingk adopted her dogs, raising pets wasn't very popular, so it was difficult to get quality food, clothing, and so on for dogs. She also wasn't so sure whether mass-produced items for dogs were safe or not. Dogs have very delicate, sensitive skin, and Tingk wanted to make comfortable, pretty clothes with soft, nice fabrics for her dogs. So she started making clothes for canines and got more and more involved in the world of crafts. She took several craft courses on clothing, Korean traditional clothing (Hanbok), and accessories. Tingk also applies her skills in quilting, felting, and other crafts to make clothes for dogs.

Now Tingk also has two cats, Hope and Shabel. She makes not only dog clothes but cat clothes and items, too. She's having a great time making pet clothes, and she posts fun entries with her dogs and cats on her blog and on Facebook. Check her out here:

tingkstyle.com
facebook.com/tingkstyle